The Need-Not Artist™

The Need-Not Artist™

KASHA RITTER

Text & Copyright Kasha Ritter

Text Edit Kim Taylor on behalf of StoryTerrace

Design StoryTerrace

First print July 2023

CONTENTS

INTRODUCTION 7

1. TALENT: NOT AN ABILITY GIFTED TO A FEW 17

2. TIME: HOW TO FIND IT AND USE IT CREATIVELY 27

3. SUPPORT: NOT AS NECESSARY AS YOU IMAGINE 39

4. INSPIRATION: IT'S INNATE. LEARN TO SUMMON IT WHEN YOU NEED IT 49

5. CONFIDENCE: A HABIT WE BUILD THROUGH OUR WORK 59

6. INTUITION: YOU KNOW MORE THAN ENOUGH TO START 69

7. MANAGEMENT: HOW TO CUT OUT THE MIDDLE MAN 79

8. FAME: YOU DEFINE YOUR SUCCESS 95

9. GO FORTH AND CREATE: SHARE YOUR VISION 107

AUTHOR'S NOTE 117

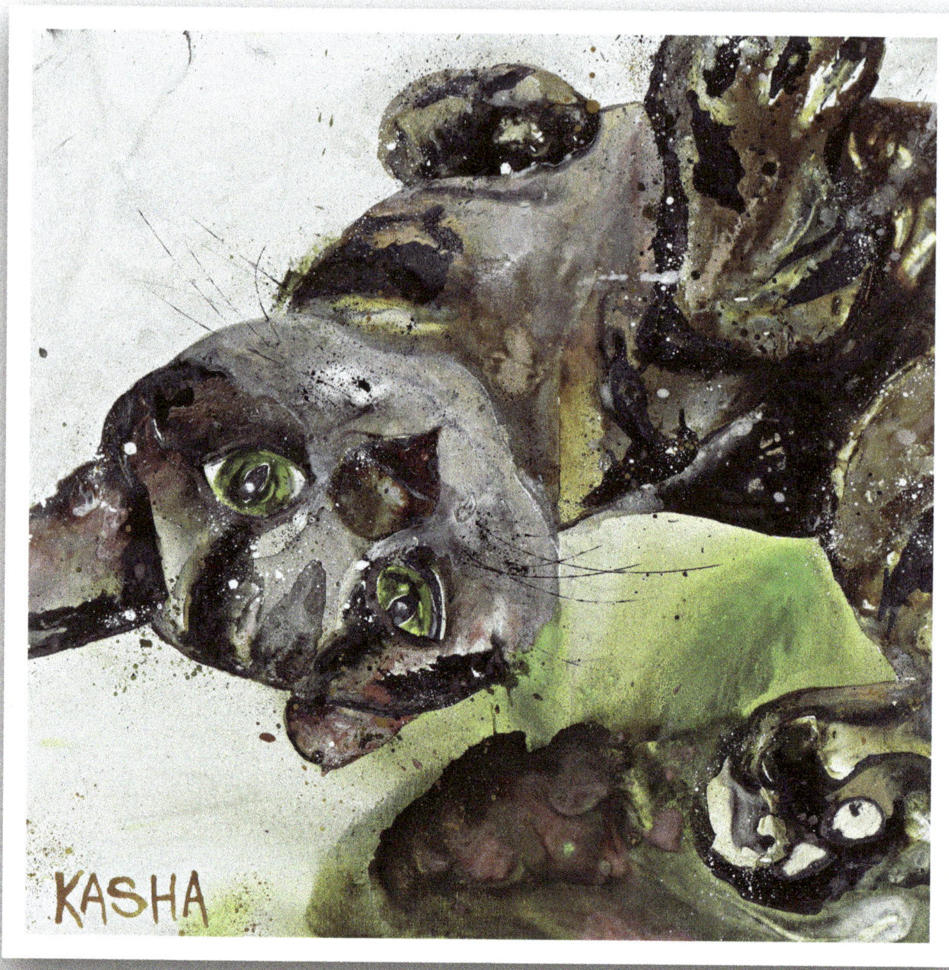

Play. Pause. 30" x30"
Meet Lola the cat who knocked ink onto canvas and taught me how to paint.

INTRODUCTION

Lola was racing at me. She was our tabby cat with big opinions. I watched as she came out of nowhere, pouncing open jars of ink and spilling them onto my canvas. I had just set up the ink and canvas on the floor, ready to paint. I was sitting there, considering how exactly to use the ink when she landed and shifted the dynamic in an instant. In shock, I desperately grabbed the jar's eye droppers to pull off the ink and put it back in its bottle. Reacting with urgency removed all thought and allowed possibility to show up. As I suctioned off the ink, the colors moved together to form what looked like a flower petal. This was my classic *ah-ha* moment. I thought I needed to be careful, focused, and deliberate, but what I really needed was to be carefree, relaxed, and casual. Most things in my life at this time had required a good deal of effort, so I assumed I needed to try hard to make art. It turned out that art was going to be an entirely different type of relationship.

This was 2008 when I had a very full life; I was happily married with three dogs and three kids, two years apart in age. While it seemed that I didn't need another thing to do, I was certain I needed art in my life. It called me back. Though I had attended a graphic art school for a year, and taken a drawing class in college, I was not classically trained in painting canvas' nor comfortable with using color. I had worked in various creative fields prior to being a stay-at-home mom but these fields were more problem-solving than intuitively connecting to creation. I was a technical illustrator, using rapidographs on vellum. I was a graphic artist, creating logos for businesses or designing menus for restaurants. This call back to art was my way of caring for and reconnecting with myself. It was important to me to think beyond the role of wife and mother. I wondered what I could bring to the world as a way of giving back to the women who had come before me, many of whom enabled me to be here now, living this life.

The lessons I learned as wife and mom impacted my relationship with art. Part of being a mom and wife is building quality relationships, which is what art has been for me: a relationship. Art has been a friend, therapist, confidante, and sparring partner. An equalizer. When I would feel inadequate in my other roles, art would remind me of my intrinsic value. When home life would be serene, art would remind me I still needed to be challenged. When home life was chaotic, art would provide a peaceful place. Sometimes art would have me on my knees, frustrated by my inability to capture a vision, and other times it seemed to paint itself. Art has played a profound part in my life. To say I am grateful sounds obligatory but this statement stems from genuine appreciation.

Looking back, it has been one of *the* most important relationships because of its ability to transform the person I believed myself to be. It has been a lifeline and a touchstone, reminding me of my basic truths. Art called upon the qualities I naturally contain while also expecting me to figure out a way to do it better, so that I could be better.

The world likes to define you and interrupt you so it can tell you who you should be. Art is my way of telling the world who I am in my own words, uninterrupted.

Being an artist can be perceived as a frivolous, silly endeavor. Pursuing art as a profession or as a hobby can be viewed as a fruitless impossibility. After fifteen years of creating artwork, the list of things this endeavor has taught me is sweetly significant. This book will share some of those simple lessons with you.

To start with, I learned to be heard and to listen. To trust and be skeptical. To be brave and bold. To pick and choose. To be persistent and patient. To start and to finish. To show up and try again. To be kind and firm with myself. I learned that creative chaos loves disciplined boundaries. I learned that what works for me is the right way. What works for you is your right way.

Art has taught me to be true to my word, and mindful of my actions. It has taught me that small details matter greatly and the big picture matters very little because the small details eventually create the big picture. I learned that even a finished piece of art that was not visually appealing often brought new insights through the process of creating it, so creating it was indeed useful and worthwhile.

Life is full of instructions, telling us what we need before we do something. "You need your coat, you're going to get cold." or "You need to be careful, you're making a mess." But maybe you like the cold and want to make a mess. This book will reframe some of those must-needed ideas into need-nots. Art has taught me I needed-not what I thought; I already had what I needed. This is the role art plays in life. It has the ability to take what you naturally are and create from the place of who you have always *been*. We forget that we are creations at our core. It is in our very essence to have a need to create because it's how we began life. Giving ourselves permission to have a relationship with art adds a depth to our humanness. We also inspire others to consider their creativity. We all look to others for inspiration in life. I'm sure you can recall someone who has done this for you possibly without them even knowing you were watching.

I ask myself two questions when I paint to stop overthinking and feel the energy of the work: what do I see, and what do I feel? For example: what I see is not a dog's nose — what I see is a round shape that has curves with light and dark shadows. What I feel is the genuine love a dog displays when she nestles her nose against your hand. That is what I paint. That is what people can see in the work: they can see that *feeling*. People would tell me they loved how my work felt. The more I heard this the more I realized they were feeling what I felt when I painted.

The act of creating is incredibly important in life. It's a way of communicating. It's a way of discussing things that sometimes are difficult to say. It's a way of expressing your truth so others can understand it. It's an intelligent energy that changes lives. Let it change yours. May this book nudge you to create your own relationship with art. May it be a book you come back to when you doubt yourself. May it be a book you share with others who need to hear what it has to say. May you have patience with yourself as you discover how you do your art.

I am quite grateful to everyone who has, who does, and who will play a role in my life, which now includes you as you read this. I thank you wholeheartedly. Please know that people need to see your art. People need to read your book. We should share what we know about what we have learned, to pay it forward and pay it backward to those who have walked us this far. Together, we learn how to fearlessly create good.

" Tame the cat-calling chaos circling your soul. Sweet talk it with tales of how what you do matters and the way you do it is vital. Then step into the grace of who you are. Work relentlessly at your craft without struggle. Remember creativity breathes in purpose not oxygen."

Kasha Ritter

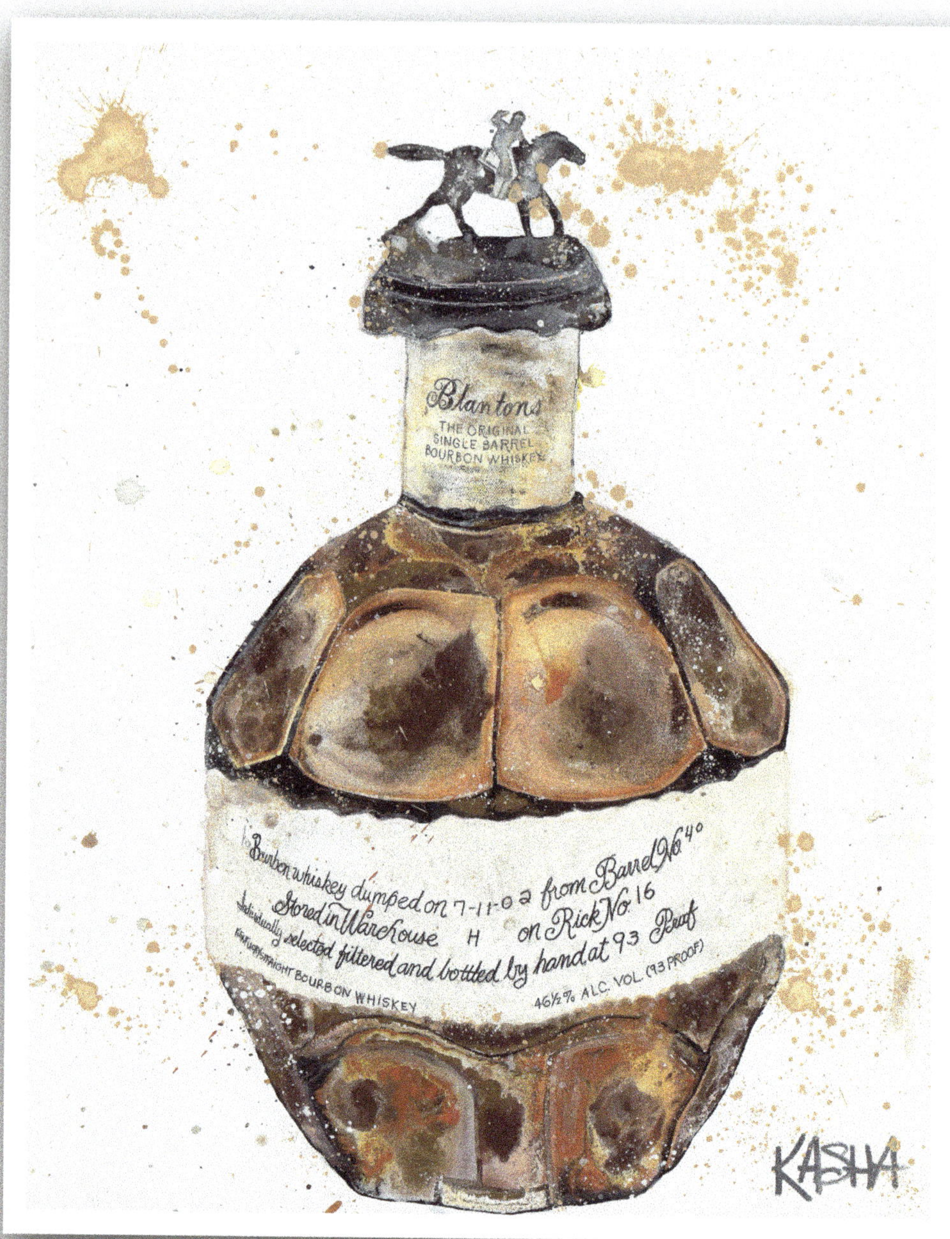

Single Barrel 36” x 24”

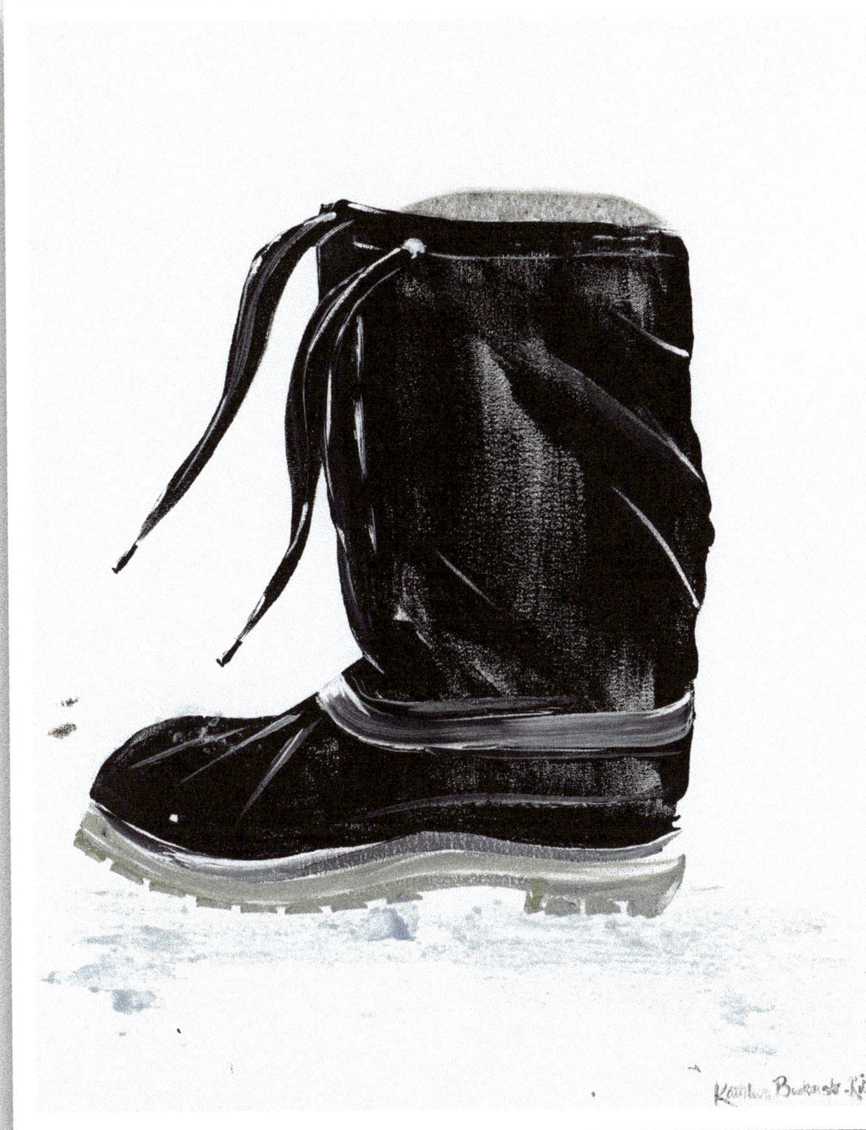

Frosted 24" x 28"
© 2010 Kasha Ritter

1

TALENT: NOT AN ABILITY GIFTED TO A FEW

You need-not talent to be an artist — you need experience, which builds it. We think talent is a special ingredient, a rare gift that artists are graced with at birth. Yes, some artists have natural abilities, but all artists work at their craft. As with any skill in life, practice is key to building talent. Practice means putting in the time with a curious mind and an open spirit. Practice is not precise and predictable but playful and possible. If you are not having fun, you won't show up to learn. Your talent is fluid. What you call talent currently will look much different a year from now than five years from now. Experience composts. It will grow out of the accumulation of time you put in. Trust where you are and enjoy your moments with art.

The artwork **Frosted** is a simple snow boot that all three of my kids wore, so it held happy memories of them conquering snowbanks with bright red cheeks — then coming in for hot chocolate to thaw out. Sweet snow days when life slowed down and we played together. Simple joy! This black boot was a touchstone for those memories, making it easy to paint as a beginner. As you start off, keep it simple. Choose things you can start, finish, and succeed at. Build your confidence. I avoided using color at first because I didn't understand it. I thought I needed to learn the correct ways to use color and to take a class on it or read books on it. I needed to keep everything simple so as to finish and learn. That's okay. Where you are now is okay too. You have enough to get started. Believe that.

My goal when painting at first was to not get something wrong. I was determined to make a painting look like a boot to prove I was good enough to be an artist. That was the mindset. I was not at ease when painting at first. "Don't mess this up." was the theme song. I had little time and money to be investing in art supplies, so it needed to be good.

The artwork **Single Barrel** would happen years later after I learned that it takes layers of ink to produce a piece and that the many mistakes I would make added to the character of the piece. In the first piece, I stayed clear of mistakes out of fear, but my later work would welcome mishaps because of the unique creative energy they embodied. Much like a good conversation that enables someone to say something randomly that can change your life, accidental events in art will transform you and your technique. Relax. It's just art.

It's also tempting to look for reasons to stop at first

because art is scary, unknown territory. We make decisions through guesswork, randomly throwing darts at our reputation, time, and money because we think we must explain ourselves to others. But guessing comes from a deep intuition, a knowing. The more we tell ourselves to keep moving forward, the clearer the path becomes. Keep saying, "Let's see what happens if I do this…." Learn as you go, as you did as a child when learning was all you did. You kept trying because you saw others had done it and believed you could, too.

Simple steps to overcome your belief that you need more talent than you have now:

1. **Believe** you'll have the future talent you envision. Look back at some current skills you have that are effortless now, but once presented a struggle. Cooking, athletic skills, playing music, writing, dancing, acting, and even learning the art of conversing all count. Remember this is how talent works, it builds. Talent in creating artwork forms in that same way.
2. **Understand** that how you will gain this experience is up to you. There isn't one way or one correct path. Some people watch videos, read books, or journal, while others take classes or simply put in hours of work by trial and error. Maybe you will do some combination. How you

learn is your art language. Banish the words "I don't know," because that is not true when creating. We may not know *exactly* but we do have a guiding intuition that takes us in a direction. Build on this. The more you can step into intuition, the clearer the direction becomes.

3. **Justify** your work to no one, for there is no need to ask permission to be an artist. You don't need to be "allowed" to be your creative self, nor is art a frivolous task. Being creative is part of who we are. We come from creation in the making, so it is natural for us to be called to create. Believe in your abilities. Trust in where you are
4. **Play. Smile. Relax.** Listen to your favorite music. Breathe out. Art is energy and movement. Your state of mind as you create is a part of your work. Others will feel what you feel when you make your art. ENJOY IT so others can, too.

Small Useful Steps to Do Now:

1. **Draw:** Drawing is putting down lines. Every letter you make is a small drawing, so your grocery list is a work of art. Drawing lines is the foundation for art, sketches, ideas, and putting shapes down on canvas. You have been drawing every day. You have this in you.
2. **See:** See how you are creative: what colors you choose to wear or have in your home, how you organize it. Creativity is a part of who you have always been. Start

noticing it.

3. **Build:** Build your creative foundation, which becomes experience to grow your talent. Please don't set rigid rules; instead, be kind to yourself and play. If you're not having fun, you won't want to create, so make it fun. Set simple daily steps for you to grow comfortable with your creativity. Maybe while you drink your morning coffee, you draw the coffee cup. Or during your lunch hour, draw what you see: a tree or a pen. Or note the things you'd like to create.

End of Chapter Checklist:

☑ **Need-not talent**: You don't need more talent than you currently have; you need *experience*, which comes from creating. Go create and build from that.

☑ **Need-not doubt:** You don't need to doubt your level of creativity, even if it feels nonexistent. Don't allow yourself to feel ill-equipped. Instead, take a moment to feel proud that you valued your call to art, and are brave enough to follow through. Be interested in what you know and will learn along the way. Take notes and photos of your work. Document your journey. Someday you might put it in a book and help others.

☑ **Need-not transform**: You don't need to change who you are as you begin your life with art. Allow the creative work to shift who you know yourself to be. You don't need to buy expensive art supplies; you can use printer copy paper and a pencil or pen. Collect all your drawings in a simple binder. I use plastic protector sleeves within a binder. Dick Blick is an online store with endless, affordable art supplies. It's unnecessary to dress or act like an artist unless doing so helps you feel creative. As you pay attention to what you see, hear, and feel while you create, and as you build your portfolio and skills, you also build the kind of artist *you* want to be.

If you liked the artwork seen in this chapter, make it your own here:

Frosted: https://kasha-ritter.pixels.com/featured/frosted-kasha-ritter.html
Single Barrel: https://kasha-ritter.pixels.com/featured/single-barrel-kasha-ritter.html

" Art is a conversation where you learn when to listen, when to speak, when to be quiet, and when to keep talking until you say what you need to say."

Kasha Ritter

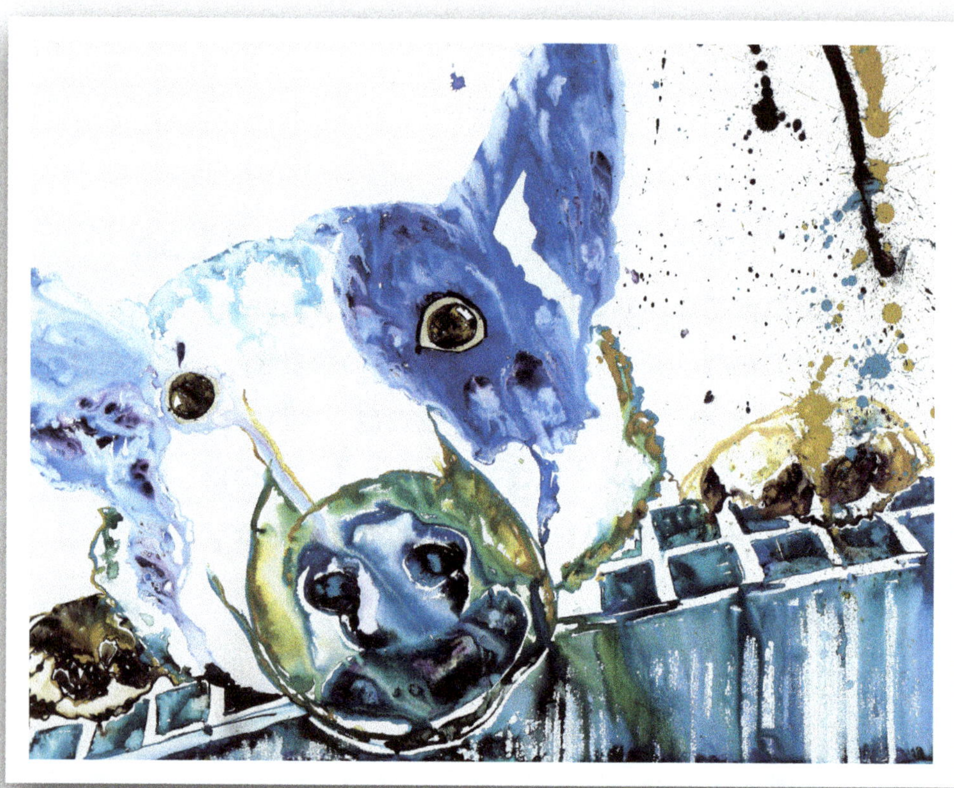

In The Beginning 48" x 60"

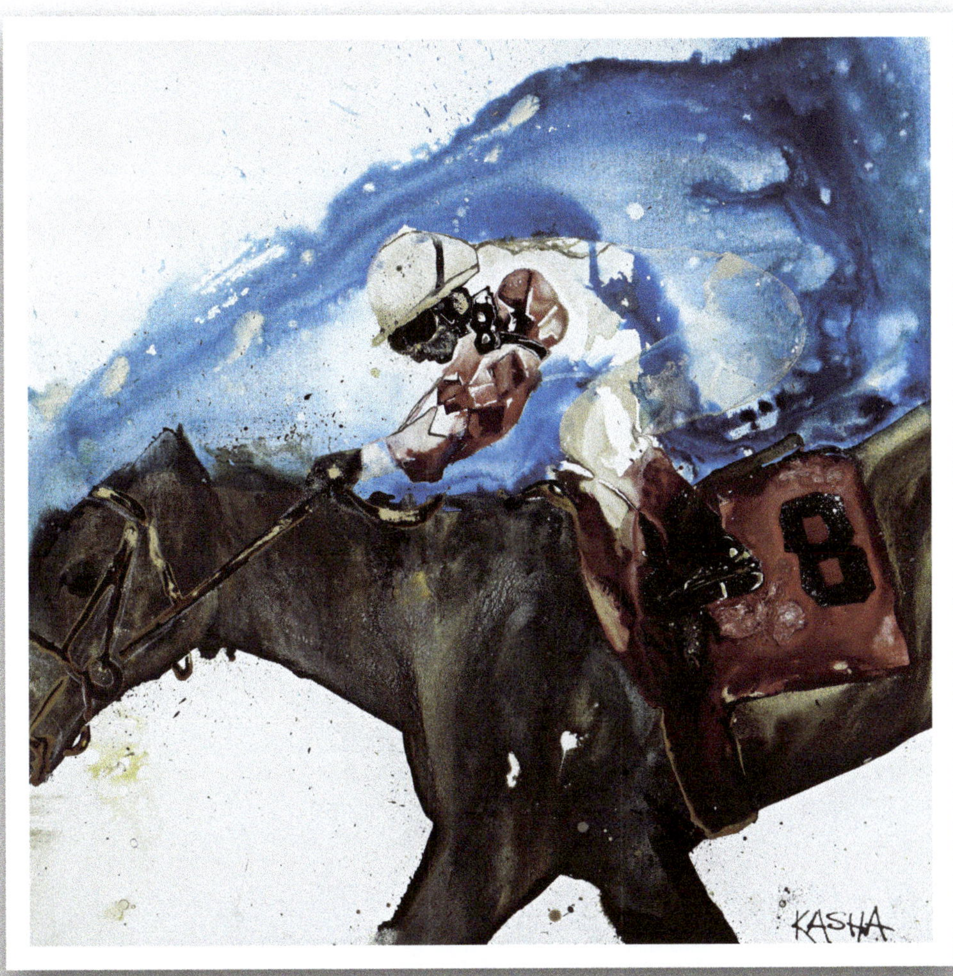

Atmospheric Pressure 30" x 30"
© 2012 Kasha Ritter

2

TIME: HOW TO FIND IT AND USE IT CREATIVELY

The artwork **In The Beginning** took a long time and was my first large piece of canvas. I was so unsure of myself I didn't sign this piece of art. The image is of our dog Zazu whose presence was innately calming. She was my spirit animal in many ways. Because I cared greatly about the subject and cared greatly about my investment with this large pieceI slowly thought about each area, worried about each section. Having no deadline, I had all the time I needed and felt stuck at one point. Should I do more? Could I do more? Am I done? Time gave me no guidance.

The artwork **Atmospheric Pressure** had a timeline. I needed to donate it to an event. Having this urgency was helpful, and you can feel it in the piece. The splashes of water and movement of color were captured. It feels more alive than the first piece. Neither way is wrong or right, but it proves that more time is not what we need. Trust that each piece you create will happen in the right amount of time. It always does. Perfection is not achieved with one piece of art, but is layered through your experience, and evolves with you.

You need-not tremendous amounts of time to create art. You need concentrated moments that produce creativity — small pockets of moments. You think you need endless uninterrupted hours to create a masterpiece. You do not. What you need is to find small pockets of time for art. Block it out, and make it happen. Day by day, week by week, you build your foundation. You get better at your craft and complete more in shorter amounts of time because you see what you can do within your windows of time. Often with less time, we do more, because the pressure forces us to focus.

The two paintings above were done in the same year but took different amounts of time. You may have children, a full or part-time job, or aging parents you care for, and feel your art would require time you don't have — yet it's something you long to do. I know that feeling. My days were full with three young children who were partially home-schooled, three dogs, and a husband who traveled. The chores were endless. I thought I needed a weekend alone to paint. What I discovered is how to seize moments to paint for 20 minutes. When I had a half hour before picking up the kids, I would create. If dinner was simmering, I would play for a bit. Little by little, layer by layer. Doing a little bit enabled me to see the work anew when I returned to it, too.

I am not an early morning artist, but it's a lovely and quiet time to create. Staying up later at night works too. In the beginning, it's challenging to prioritize your art because it feels like you're neglecting other things. I urge you to reframe that. You are investing in yourself, which makes you better. Think of creativity as a vitamin that makes you happy, brings you joy, fulfills your heart, makes you laugh, relaxes your brain, and rewires your mind. Just as you eat good food and exercise for a healthy body-mind connection, taking the time to create contributes to a healthy mindset. Creating art enables us to step back from the stressful demands of life to reset. The dirty kitchen floor and endless emails will be there when you're finished making art. Take the time.

I was forced to take the time to draw 51 years ago around the age of seven. I was terrorizing my brothers, so my grandmother, Nanny, pulled me aside and she said, "Sit down and draw me something." When I finished, she hung my drawing up on the fridge. It was a sign that what I drew mattered. It made her happy. She may have been happy because she thought I did a good job, or she may have been relieved that I stopped pushing my brothers off their bikes. The drawing was a small elephant that I traced with a stencil. I lost track of time, since drawing felt familiar. Somehow drawing knew me or knew something about me, much like Nanny knew something about me. I owe my life with art to her.

As I grew older, art was where I felt truly understood. I returned to art years later at a time when I often felt misunderstood. Raising children can be full of chaos when they're young, then confusion and misunderstandings when they're teenagers, and I spent a lot of effort trying to avoid misunderstandings in the household. When I would paint, regardless of what I put down on canvas, it felt okay. I didn't have to explain myself. Art asked nothing of me and was just happy I showed up. I still feel that way when I paint: creating comprehends the whole of me. When I paint there's a communication between myself and the medium —a tacit sense that we know each other. The small act of taking time to be more than a wife and a mom enabled me to transition out of full-time motherhood much easier when the kids left the nest because I had forged this relationship with art. Creating art also recreates who you are. It gives back to you in subtle yet profound ways.

Simple Steps to Discover Time for Your Art in Hidden Places:

1. **Slip art into your schedule.** My laundry trick is one example, and if you work in an office, you might take a coffee break in the afternoon and sketch, or go outside and sketch, or snap photos of things you want to paint. Have some art supplies in your car, and during lunch, dive in. Give yourself a half hour before bed. The time

you devote to your craft pays off in ways you can't imagine when first starting. You learn, create more, and build confidence. Art is a touchstone to remember who you are and what you value.

2. **Sync:** View time and life as working with you, not against you, and it will make a difference. You'll see that life is constantly providing time for your art, even if it's not long stretches of time. If you believe you can do more with less, you'll feel less stressed.
3. **Salted:** It's such a simple metaphor, to salt something. A little bit accentuates the experience. The right amount satisfies. Too much overwhelms. The same is true of time and creativity. Trust that every moment you invest will grow in compound interest.
4. **System:** Have your own unique system behind everything you do as you begin your life with art. Keep tasks streamlined and simple. I have three major steps to any system, then I expand from that.

   #1. I put down big blocks of color across the canvas, as you would fill in a coloring book. NO details at this step: just block out color.

   #2. I go back in with layers of more color, tying it together, looking at how colors next each other interplay and can layer over each other. A bit more detail here.

   #3. Now I come back in and draw lines to define areas, create definite spaces on top of the ink and splatter color to highlight and add texture. I start big and wide, then I narrow down. Find a system that works for you. 1, 2, 3. Simple.

Small, Useful Steps to Do Now:

1. **Bundle:** If you have small children, let them do their artwork as you do yours. Make it clear that you need to concentrate, and so do they. If they're watching a movie, work on your art for 90 minutes. Give them a stack of books. You can fold your art time in with office meals and breaks. Do you talk on the phone? Have a sketch pad nearby for long conversations. Enjoy the process of learning how to be more creative.
2. **Create:** Start seeing the ways you can reorganize your time for art. Streamline your home and office schedules to create time for even 30-minute sessions. Apply your creativity to the task: if you spend 30 to 45 minutes a day prepping family meals, then make the next day's meal prep in advance. You may even prep a few days in advance and use the freezer more often. Create!
3. **Expand:** Once you've grown used to carving out time for art, it will become more natural. From there, you'll shape your future. Don't stress or push it, simply go with what you can do, when you can do it. Know that the rest will unfold. This is how you gain experience: you expect it. There will be something familiar even in

uncharted territory. Gravitate towards that. Strengthen that.

End of Chapter Checklist:

- ☑ **Need-not time:** You don't need more time than you currently have — you need to creatively find moments within your day to devote to your art. You don't need to feel pressure to create more time for yourself, instead streamline your schedule to find time. It's there, hiding within your day, and obvious when you seek it.
- ☑ **Need-not doubt:** You don't need to worry about the amount of time it requires to create artwork. You can create in small increments over the course of a week or a month. All your efforts add up. Sometimes slower is better because it gives you time to grow with your work.
- ☑ **Need-not transform:** You won't need to extend your hours or overhaul your life in ways that seem unreasonable. Take small steps and delve in as your schedule permits. As you find your rhythm and increase your output, you'll also gain the confidence to sell your art, then eventually, if you desire, to do artwork full-time. When you take time for your art you learn and grow in ways that are immeasurable, both as an artist and as a person.

If you liked the artwork seen in this chapter, make it your own here:

In The Beginning: https://kasha-ritter.pixels.com/featured/in-the-beginning-kasha-ritter.html
Atmospheric Pressure: https://kasha-ritter.pixels.com/featured/atmospheric-pressure-kasha-ritter.html

"Did you lose track of time?
Then you've found what you
are meant to do.
You have to forget who you
are. You have to be willing
to be led astray."

Kasha Ritter

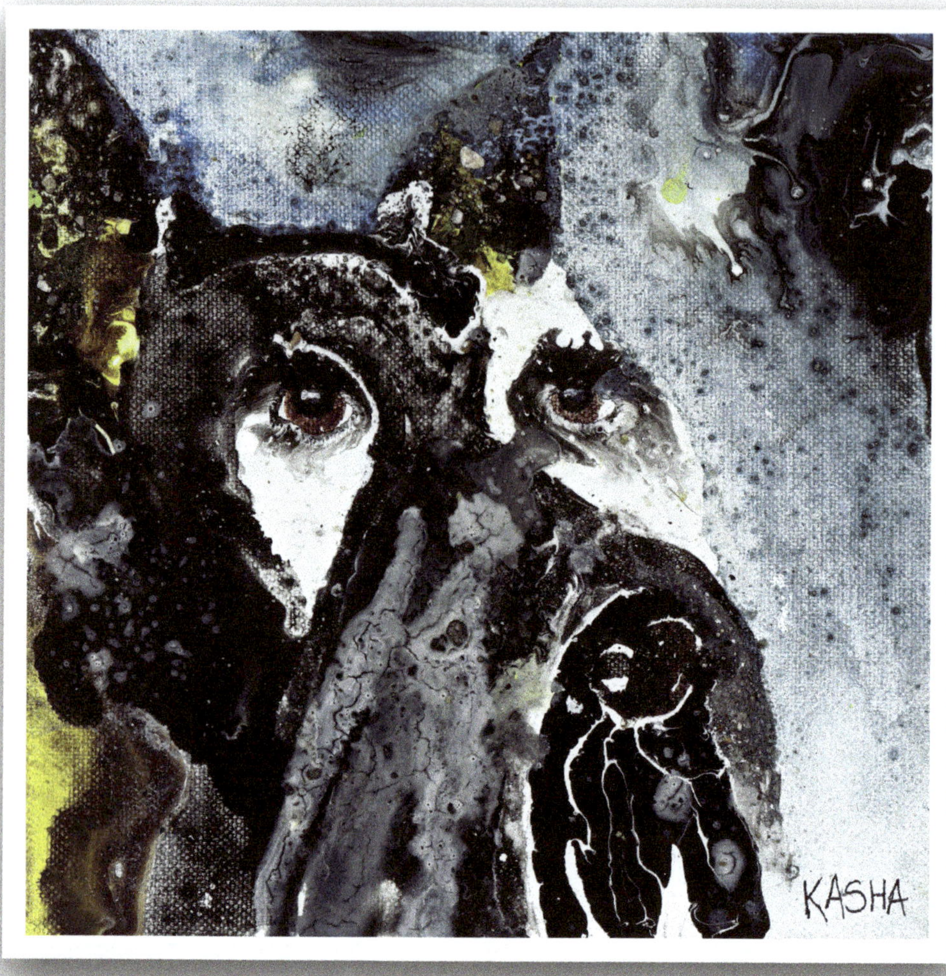

Scott. Tea 10" x 10"
© 2012 Kasha Ritter

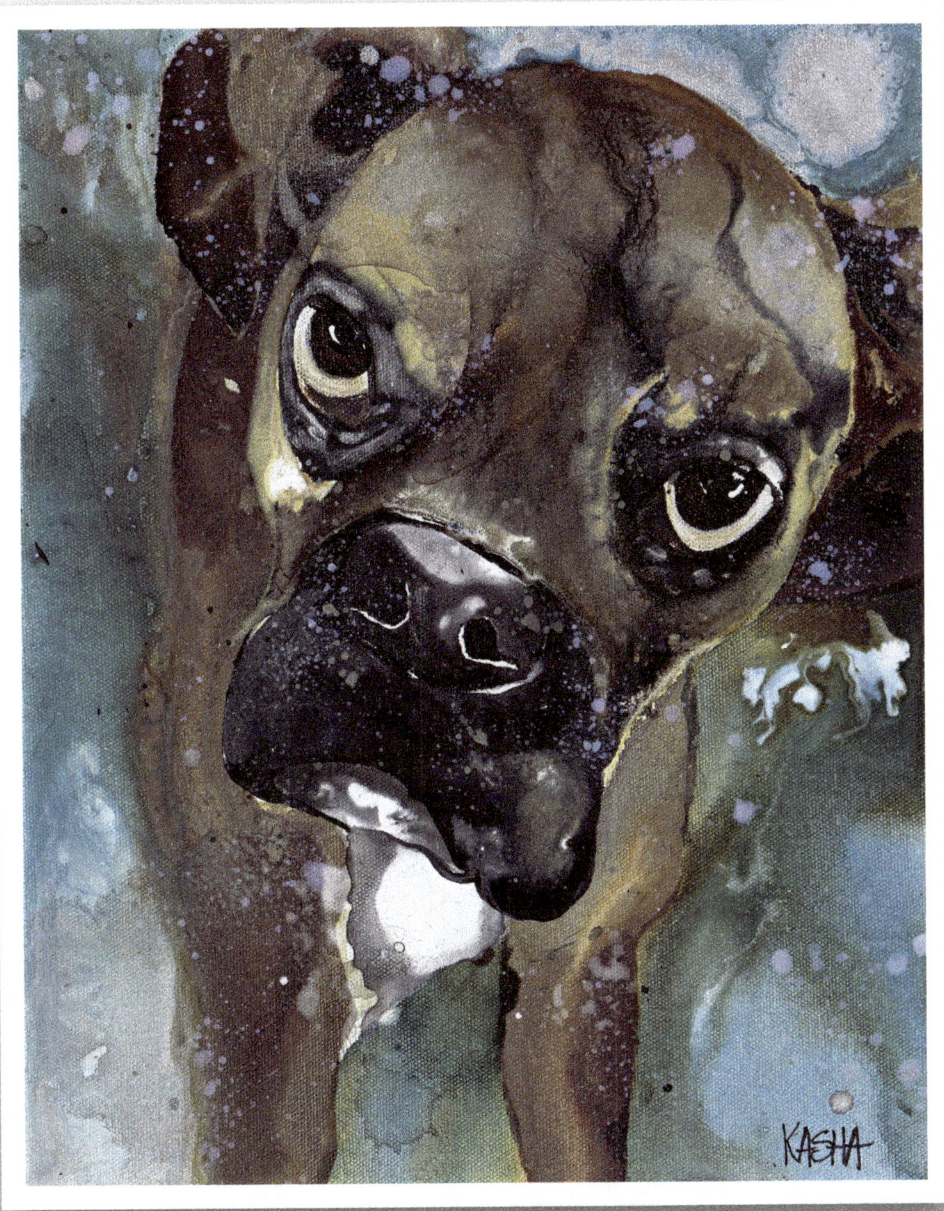

Miss Maya 12" x 9"

3

SUPPORT: NOT AS NECESSARY AS YOU IMAGINE

The artwork **Scott. Tea** was done quickly. It was a small canvas with a small amount of paint. It felt crowded to me, immediately, because the dimensions did not allow room to move around. This made me feel unsteady and unsupported because I had found a familiar comfort in painting larger pieces of canvas. This compact piece is nothing remarkable, but it is a part of my story and again holds a valuable lesson for me. I still gained experience. I learned to work with what I had, and as with all of the art we create, I now have a memory of that moment in time. And I didn't need support to create this, so much as time.

The artwork **Miss Maya** was a commission. I had an art space where I could leave the work set up and return to it. I had money to invest in needed supplies, knowing it was a paid job, along with a profit to invest back into the business. This fueled my confidence, making it a breeze to paint this pup with her adorable attitude. That joy and confidence produced a piece of artwork the customer loved. You can see how these aspects feed into each other.

To have a relationship with art, you need-not extra support. You need to create systems that will support making your art. You need a designated space and to move casual spending money into your art supply fund. When we consider beginning something new, we look to others to confirm that it's right. The problem is, our dream may not resonate with them. Self-support is where you find your validation. Assure yourself that *you* know what you want, and you have what you need. Discover what that means to you.

In prioritizing your art, you need a designated space to work. A space where you can leave things set up so you can jump in and work. It does not need to be large or even to have a door, it just needs to be *your* space. My first studio was in the kids' playroom in the basement. I hung two shower curtains on a rope across the room, making a wall and door. Duct tape was placed across the carpet as a line not to be crossed. I told my kids that when the curtain was closed, they had to knock because I was working. Most of the time they played just outside the curtain. I could make a mess, clean it up, set up for the next time, and leave knowing I could return to it.

If you need money for art supplies, then other things like grabbing a coffee, moisturizer, or magic shampoo for perfect hair can wait. Choose to invest in your work. Savings add up quickly when we don't buy bottled water or coffee we can brew at home. Don't think "I will never be able to buy these things again," but view it as a shift in your priorities. Let art change your life.

It's frightening to be an artist at times, to stand alone making decisions when you feel uncertain. It's tempting to rely on others to fill that gap of unknowing, but if they fill it, then it's not yours. While others can offer support, it's necessary to navigate art on your own, in your own way. This is how you own it, and how it transforms you. This is part of the journey.

Feel deeply. Be scared. Get frustrated. Scream. Cry. Laugh. Figure it out. It's a part of the process when you put color on canvas. It's normal to hesitate and doubt yourself. Override that. Put down the ink. Remind yourself that art is layers of color and motion on canvas, which allows each moment to come together in the finished piece. Being afraid is not a signal to stop, but to take action. Step towards it. Eliminate the fear and see your artwork come to life.

Small Useful Steps to Self-Support Your Life With Art:

1. **Solution:** Find a solution for any problem you face. Wondering where to paint uninterrupted? Find a closet, basement corner, or garage. Don't feel the need to explain, just do it. If anyone questions it, tell them it's something you've always wanted to do, then change the

subject. This is your journey. Honor that space and time and what it brings to your life.

2. **Systems***:* Create your own systems, including how you set up your space, the steps you take to paint (music, candles, earbuds for concentration), and how you support yourself (affirmations, mantras). What gets you into the creative zone - music, audiobooks, silence? I do a variety of things depending on my mood and what I'm painting. There is no right or wrong way, there is only you creating your relationship with art.
3. **Saving:** This is not just about saving money, but also time and energy. Move money away from coffee and lunch and into your art fund. Move cleaning time into creative time. We know how time evaporates on social media, so move that time toward your art.
4. **Say Yes:** I went to a creative intuitive therapist early on and asked her if I should be an artist. Her answer was, "Yes, Yes, Yes!" I loved that she said it three times. Once was what everyone says, two times and we start to believe it, but to hear it three times is making a wish. Which I did, and it worked. As you delve in and do your own work, use kind and encouraging words for yourself, as though you're speaking to a small child or a puppy. We criticize ourselves as protection from what others might say. That ends now. Say, "Wonderful, wonderful, wonderful!" And "Proud of you, proud of you, proud of you!" and watch it benefit you and your art. Your words matter.

Simple Steps to Do Now:

1. **Set-Up:** Choose your art space, no matter how small. You can change it later but set it up this week.
2. **Sit-Down:** Don't overthink what you will paint, and how you'll create. Sit down. Tune in. Play. Be kind and say nice things to yourself. Have fun. Clean up afterward, so you're ready to go next time.
3. **Search:** Find something in your closet that feels like art clothing, something you're willing to get paint on. Go to a thrift store to find something. This will be your uniform to get your mindset ready to create. I still have sweatpants from years ago and yes, they are layered with paint and memories.

End of Chapter Checklist:

☑ **Need-not Doubt:** You will discover ways to support yourself once you begin looking. At first, it may feel odd to be taking away from things that are part of your routine, but you are redirecting, investing, and building. Don't doubt what you are being pulled to do. Love yourself enough to support this dream.

☑ **Need-not Stress:** Supporting a life with art doesn't require huge shifts and rearranging. Start small if that's all that is possible, but start. Find creative solutions to support your need for space, time, money, and encouragement. Have fun with it!

☑ **Need-not Fix:** Where and how you do things will change as you grow as an artist. We are not looking for the finale, we are looking for traction. Painting on the floor in a corner for now? Fine. Next, get a card table with a tablecloth for spills. Only able to reroute ten dollars a week? Perfect! In a few months that might be more. The plan you put into action is not the final plan. Your plan is creative and ever-changing, just like your art.

If you liked the art in this chapter, make it your own here:

Scott.Tea:https://kasha-ritter.pixels.com/featured/scotttea-kasha-ritter.html
Miss Maya: https://kasha-ritter.pixels.com/featured/miss-maya-kasha-ritter.html

" She finally accepted that life was always trying to work with her, not against her. And this made all the difference."

Kasha Ritter

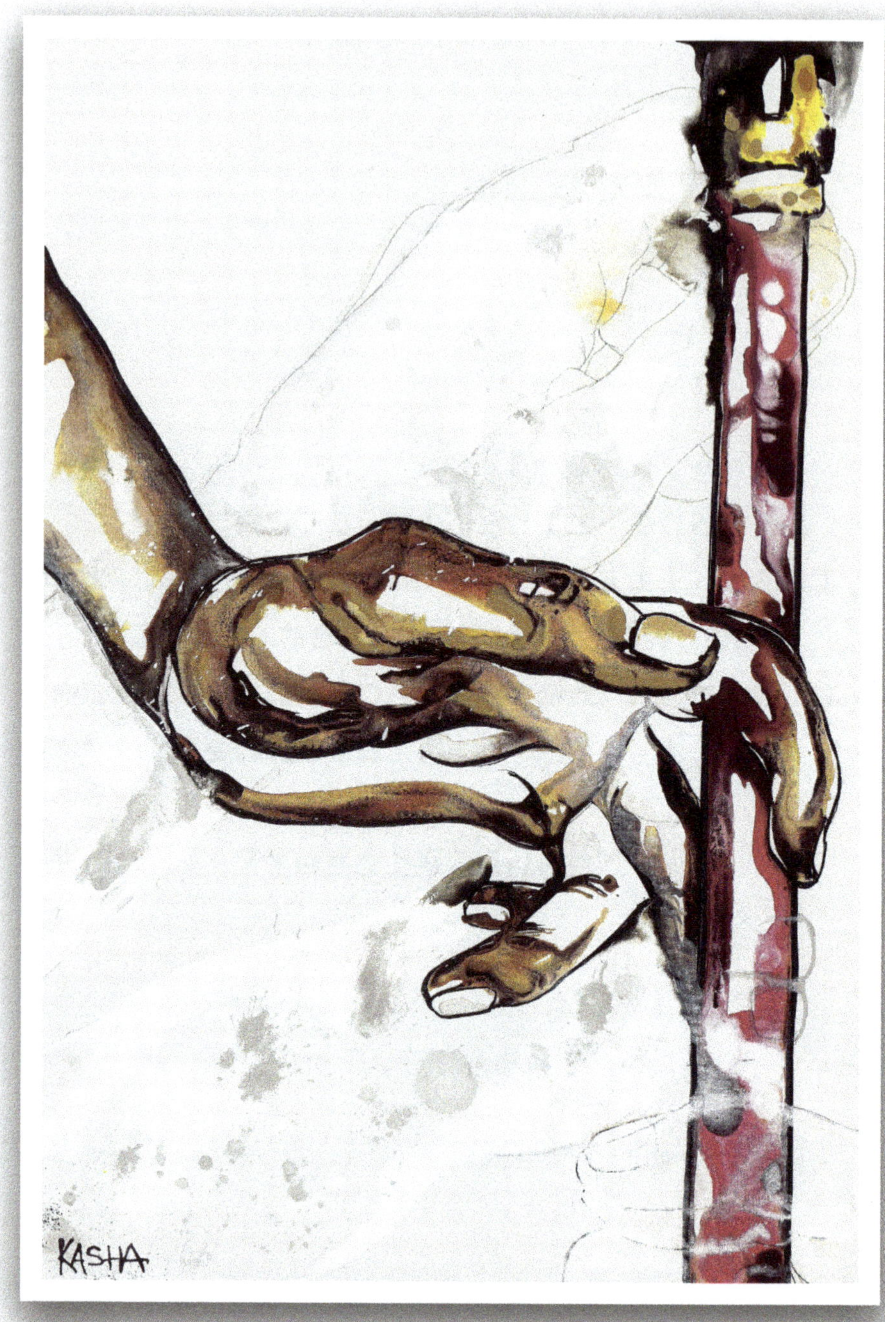

Barely Holding On 36" x 24"

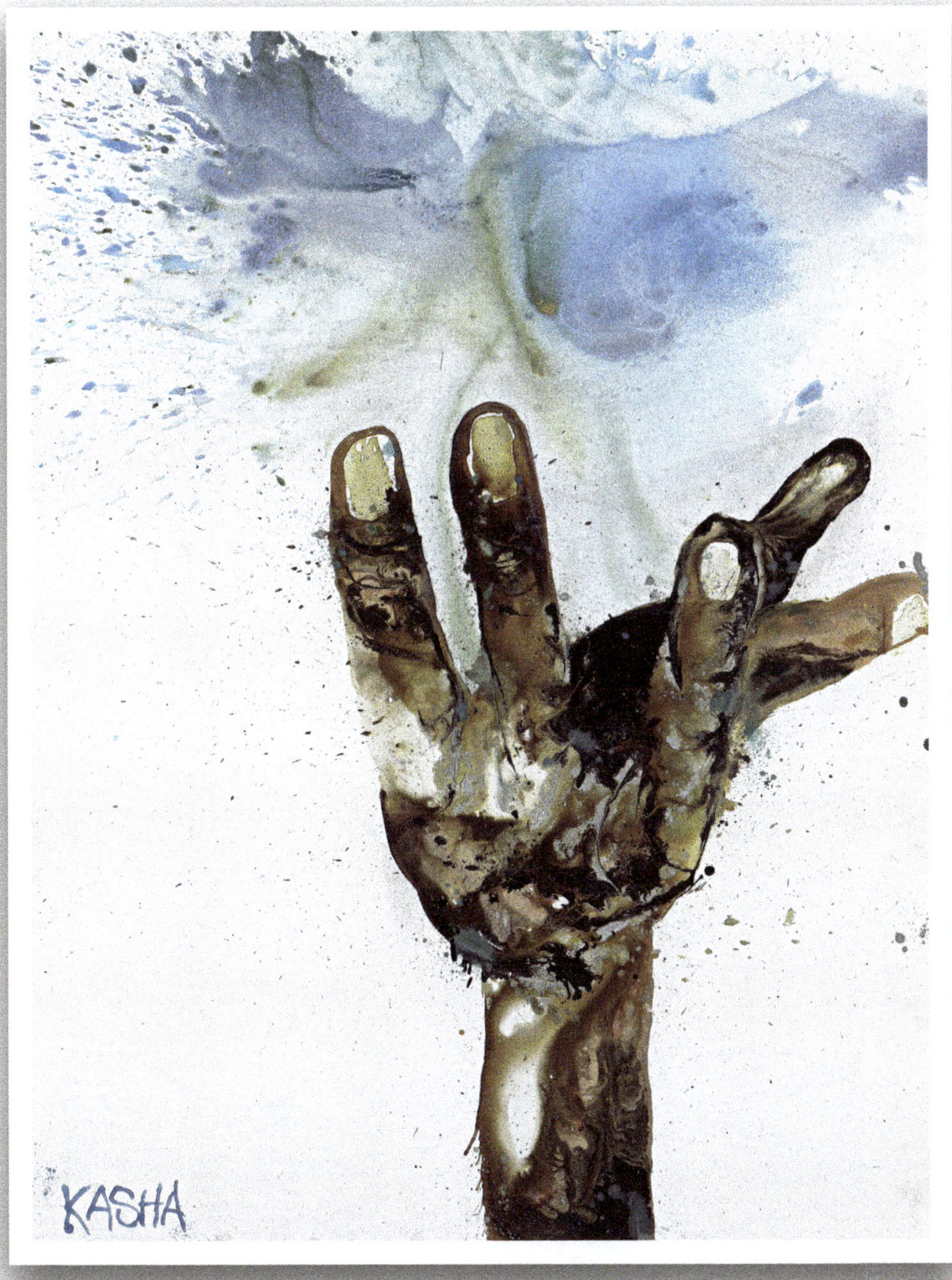

Leggo 40" x 30"
© 2011 Kasha Ritter

4

INSPIRATION: IT'S INNATE. LEARN TO SUMMON IT WHEN YOU NEED IT

The artwork **Barely Holding On** was based on a feeling and an observation; I was exhausted after sweeping the kitchen floor numerous times each day — after meals, and after kids and dogs would trash it. It occurred to me while sweeping that the broom knew more about me than most people. It knew how I felt sweeping, what I muttered, what I was thinking. I realized the act of sweeping felt useless, yet at the same time, the consistency of the task during a crazy day helped me hang on when I was barely holding it together.

The artwork **Leggo** was inspired by my love of hands. When I was a child, I would watch the hands of loved ones as they did things for me: my mom, my grandmother, my father. Their hands were all so different. Some small and smooth, some big and scarred, most wrinkled by years of work. But these hands were the delivery system for so much goodness in my life: food, sleep, help with schoolwork, hair brushing, clean clothes, a hug. It's easy to be inspired by hands when there is so much feeling behind them. With my basic system of how I create, I was able to translate what I feel for hands onto canvas — taking that feeling and turning it into inspiration to do the work, but also for those who will view it.

You need-not have intense inspiration for a life with art. You need an understanding of creativity and a feeling for how your creativity works. Artists are often asked about what inspires them or how they stay inspired. We think divine inspiration fuels productivity, but it's more like knowing *how* to be inspired. You fear that when you are not innately inspired, you cannot work. This is a misunderstanding. Inspiration is everywhere when you know how to forge it into art.

When I look at a tree I know the steps I would take to turn it into a painting. I have my system for working on canvas. I put down an outline drawing in watercolor pencil because that line will melt away once I add water. I fill in large areas I have outlined with blocks of solid colors, leaving a small space in between each area so the ink doesn't bleed together. After that dries, I add layers of ink in different colors to merge the large areas together and add depth. That dries, then I use an acrylic ink pen to outline things, literally drawing attention to sections. Lastly, I take a deep breath, choose a spot, and splatter paint in large dumps and tiny droplets. Because I understand how to use creativity, inspiration is anywhere. When you add emotion, inspiration is marked with your unique feeling, fusing what you feel with your art.

My first introduction to inspiration was at the local library in Manville, NJ, where I grew up. I was helping my little brother find a book to read when I saw *Harold and the Purple Crayon*. It was the combination of the book's purple cover and a drawing of Harold with his crayon that spoke to me. My grandmother, Nanny, had just gotten me hooked on crayons and so I felt this little guy was my new best friend. I still have the book and read it regularly. As I read the book I felt a world of possibilities open up. Harold could draw on walls and not get in trouble! I couldn't imagine a world like that! In my world drawing on walls would mean getting into huge trouble, but I could see doing what Harold was doing on paper, on the sidewalk with chalk, or even on a chalkboard, because what he did was draw into life the things he wanted to experience.

As you begin your art journey, you will have days when inspiration takes you by the hand and effortlessly leads you — and there will be days or periods of time when you can't find that kind of inspiration. But you can create it. As you begin a life with art, realize you are creating all aspects of it: how you work, what you want to communicate, how you are inspired, and what gets you to finish a piece. You know what you can't live without, and what speaks to you with certainty. Create your inspiration from this.

Small Useful Steps to Create Your Inspiration for Art:

1. **Feel:** A good deal of our life, we try to not feel too deeply. To create your inspiration for art, you need to feel fully and pay attention to what you feel and why. Talk to it. Let it answer. See how that conversation can be put on canvas and felt anew. Feeling is the core of inspiration.
2. **Realize:** To be inspired is not a random event, but a skill set. Being impressed is a part of being inspired. Are you impressed by the beauty of a sunflower? Then you are also inspired. How can you put that into a work of art for others to see and feel?
3. **Understand:** Life begs us to come to an understanding of things. We do this individually, in our own unique way. Behind many aspects of life, we discover a system, making it easier to comprehend why and how it works. Investigate what moves you to feel something, and where you take notice of it. This feeling is your foundation for your inspiration.
4. **Invest:** There will be times when inspiration is nowhere to be found. That's okay, but the work still needs to be done. Put in the work and do your best for your client or for the future famous artist you will be. Invest now and allow the inspiration to build.

Simple Steps to Do Now:

1. **Notice:** Are you irritated making salad for dinner again? Notice that feeling and take a closer look at the vegetables for potential inspiration. Are you overjoyed by a flower bed in full bloom? Take a picture to remember it. Note the feeling and ask yourself why it's emotional for you. See how this information for inspiration runs throughout your life.
2. **Plan:** Organize the steps you like to take as you create and apply them to things that grab your attention. Keep the list short so you can remember it. When you see a breathtaking sunset, for example, follow the steps in your head as to how you would paint it. Practice that mentally and see how inspiration flows.
3. **Observe:** Watch how someone with a new puppy has such a full heart. See how kids are determined, emotional, and direct. Can you feel these and use them in your work? Borrow from life where you can, since people, animals, and nature can inspire if we take time to notice.

End of Chapter Checklist:

- ☑ **Need-not monumental inspiration to be an artist.** You can be inspired by the subtleness of the wind gently blowing just as much as a tornado tearing through a landscape. It's the effect of awareness that inspires.
- ☑ **Need-not wait for inspiration to grace your presence.** You learn to call up your ability to be inspired by knowing how you will recreate something that moves you in life.
- ☑ **Need-not avoid working when you feel less inspired.** Less is often more. One line can change the entire look of a painting and is all that is needed. Don't underestimate the importance of you moving in the moment to do what needs to be done, however big or small.

If you liked the artwork in this chapter, make it your own here:

Barely Holding On: https://kasha-ritter.pixels.com/featured/barely-holding-on-kasha-ritter.html?newartwork=true
Leggo: https://kasha-ritter.pixels.com/featured/leg-go-kasha-ritter.html?newartwork=true

" She didn't always demand motivation from herself. Sometimes she whispered,
it's okay,
just try."

Kasha Ritter

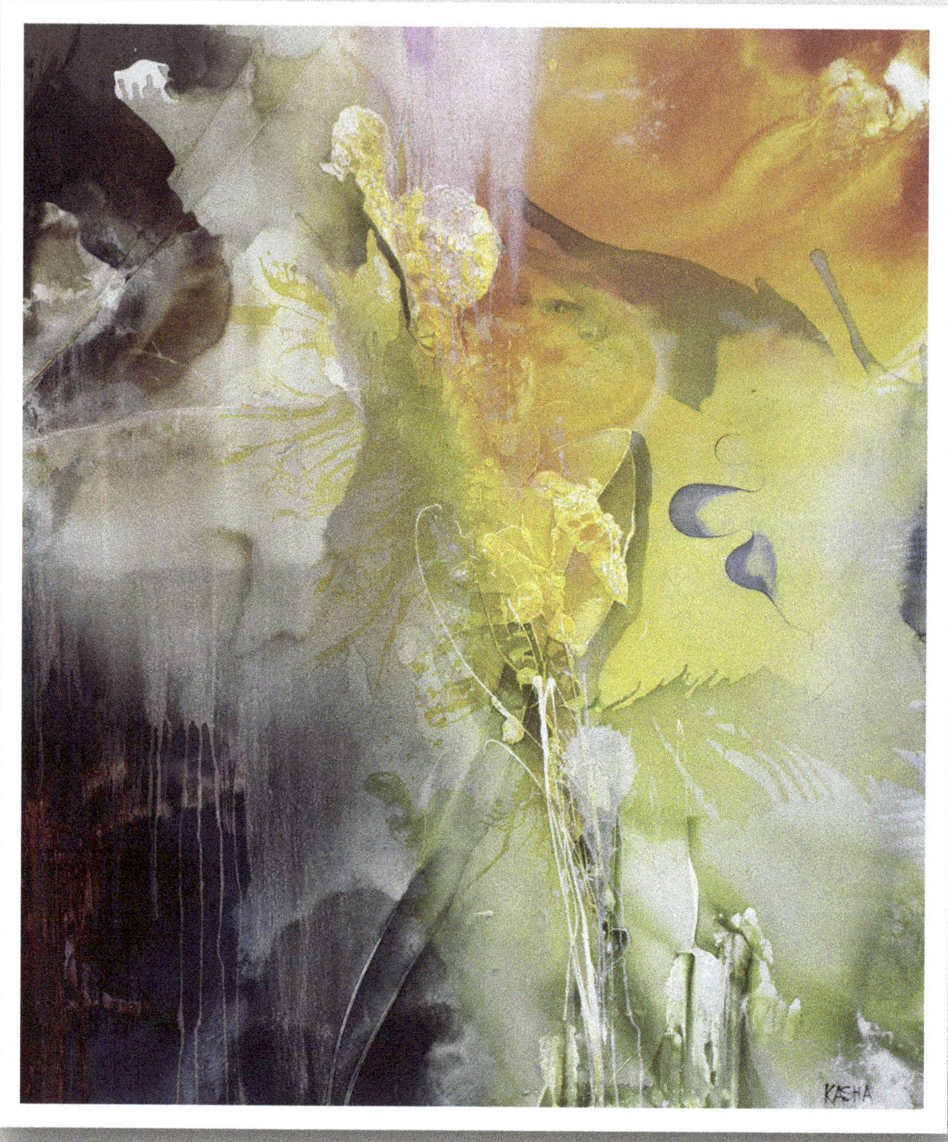

Surge 60" x 48"
© 2013 Kasha Ritter

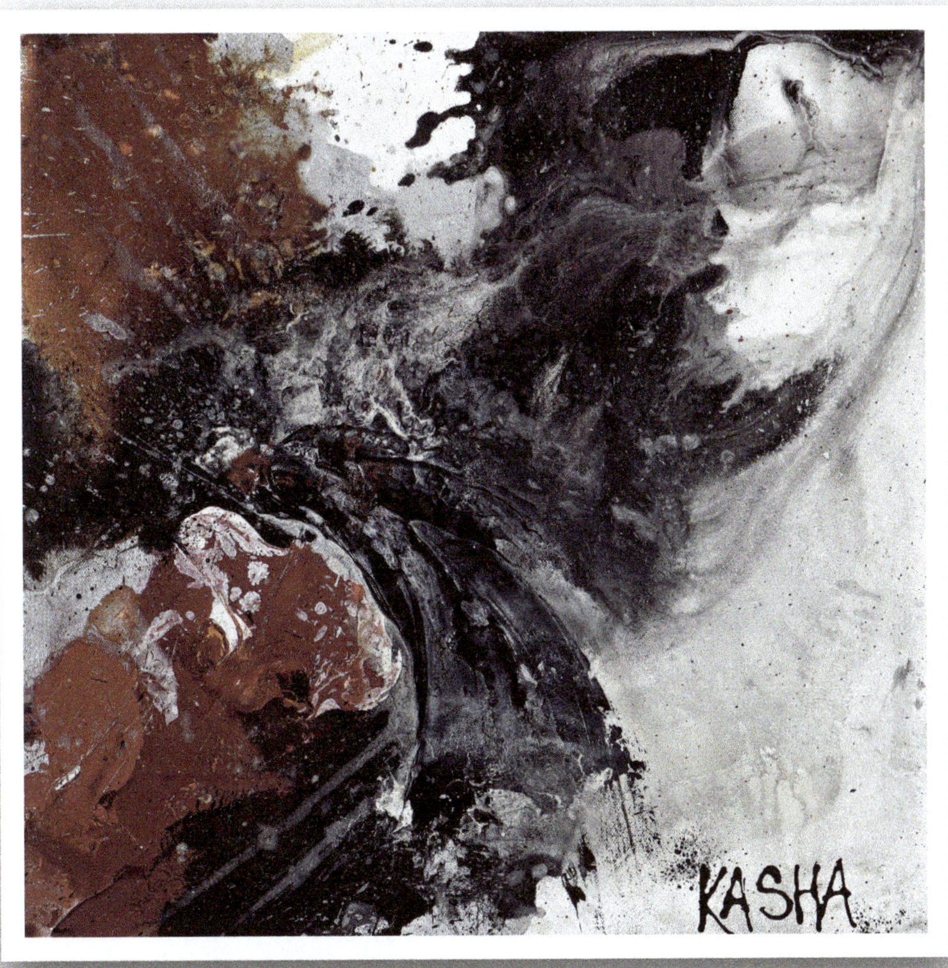

Whiplash 24" x 24"
© 2011 Kasha Ritter

5

CONFIDENCE: A HABIT WE BUILD THROUGH OUR WORK

The artwork **Surge** is full of solid decisions, one section at a time, one color at a time, one direction at a time. Abstract art is a good test of your decisiveness because there are no definite boundaries. There's no shape of a dog's head for you to paint accurately, there is only empty space, feeling, and color. In this piece, I learned I cannot decide the whole thing at once; I must make one decision at a time to see what feels right next. I can only know what to do after I watch what has happened with the first decision. How did the color move? Where did it dry? What color would work with that? That's the fun of it.

When painting the artwork **Whiplash** I hesitated to make decisions, so I limited it to three colors and avoided extra layers to reduce the stress. The decision I made was to toss down the black, add the red to balance it, then add water with white ink to blur a bit of gray. Very simple. Which, at the time, was perfect. I made decisions, I kept working, and I got better at it.

You need-not have complete confidence to find your way with art. You need the ability to decide what the next step is, even when uncertain. By making decisions, confidence is built. A misunderstood aspect of art is that an artist absolutely knows what comes next. We think their assuredness is rooted in complete confidence in their ability. This is not true. Creating art is moving ideas and energy through space, and that energy is moving while we're moving with it. How the paint moves across the canvas today will be very different from how it moves tomorrow because the energy in the moment will be different. An artist doesn't look for reliability in how the work gets done but trusts their intuition as they make decisions. Their job is to be a conduit for creativity and the connection must be certain amidst immense uncertainty.

We hesitate to decide because we desperately want to know what the *right* way is, because we think if we know that, we can be successful. But creating art is not like math or a language with set rules. Making art is more like science, where you have a hypothesis to prove. You may wonder: which is the right paint, canvas, paintbrush? What image should I paint, and when is the painting done? How will I find my style? You want these answers and many others so you don't get it wrong, but you cannot get it wrong. Will you make what appear to be mistakes? Yes. Will you dislike what you have created? At times, yes. Will you get confused and frustrated? Sure. But if you keep showing up, deciding, trusting your instincts, and honoring what you value, you are doing it the right way. Remember that it's part of the process, and your art needs you to find your voice, which is how you find your style. Making a decision is how you do that. "I don't know," is not an answer, it's a defense mechanism. When you're afraid, take control anyway. A confident decision forges a confident artist.

Let go of the need to label everything you do as right or wrong. Don't judge every line you put down or each color you pick. Allow the work to come together as you decide things. Once the artwork is done, you will see it more clearly. You'll see lessons learned, new techniques discovered, and you can keep what worked for the next piece. Any choice made as you work is perfect because it teaches, delivers new awareness, and builds skill sets. Confidence is created each time you make a definite choice and respect your decision.

But first, make those decisions. If you're unsure, decide anyway. Unhappy with what you chose? Make a different decision next time — not a better decision, because you made the best one you could in that moment. Trust. Decide. Work. Repeat.

Simple Steps to Create Confidence with Your Artwork.

1. **See:** Your choice doesn't need to be labeled right or wrong. It's neither. It's movement. Often it won't be clear what the result is until the work is completed. It's always good because you learn.
2. **Devote**: Find areas where you can practice making swift decisions: which clothes to wear, a restaurant entree, colors to use when you paint. Practice making a quick decision and leaving it alone. Support yourself positively with pride. Second-guessing pulls you backwards.
3. **Teach**: As an artist, you are both the student and the teacher. Learn to switch between these roles. When you are having a hard time deciding, become the teacher and make the choice for the good of the student.
4. **Imagine**: Play with seeing how things work out in your head. When you need to choose between two colors, take a moment, look at the canvas and imagine what each color would look like once applied. Then go with the one that feels best.

Small Useful Steps to Do Now:

1. **Inhale:** Inhale deeply and exhale as you continue to move the ink or paint across the canvas. Putting breath behind your movement allows for stability and a quiet boldness that grows fearlessness.
2. **Emote:** Use emotion in your work. It will move you to apply color in a genuine way that holds the energy of that emotion in the finished product. Joy. Happiness. Frustration. Sadness. Whatever the piece calls for, feel it as you create it. As you allow yourself to be authentic, you grow your confidence.
3. **Move**: Keep moving. It's tempting to stop to consider and criticize. Hesitate to then hang on to finding perfection. Resist that urge and keep moving. Inhale, exhale, move and work. Play music. Listen to a book on tape. Keep the energy moving forward.

End of Chapter Checklist:

☑ **Need-not certainty in every aspect as you create**. You need faith that there is a part of you that will know in the moment what to do, because you will. This is your creativity talking to you. Listen.

☑ **Need-not have the precise words** for why you move in a direction or choose what you do when you create. You need-not explain yourself to others, only to believe in yourself as an artist. You need not permission or allowance to do this.

☑ **Need-not rate your level of confidence or lack of it,** on any scale that you think exists. This is unnecessary and unhelpful. There is no need for you to hurry in this process. What is important is that you hear your creative voice and honor that. There is no finish line to meet. Enjoy the journey.

If you liked the artwork in this chapter, make it your own here:

Surge: https://kasha-ritter.pixels.com/featured/1-surge-kasha-ritter.html?newartwork=true
Whiplash: https://kasha-ritter.pixels.com/featured/whiplash-kasha-ritter.html

" It's hard not to question yourself as you try to stay on track with creating. There's always that need to be aware of direction until you remember that art is not linear."

Kasha Ritter

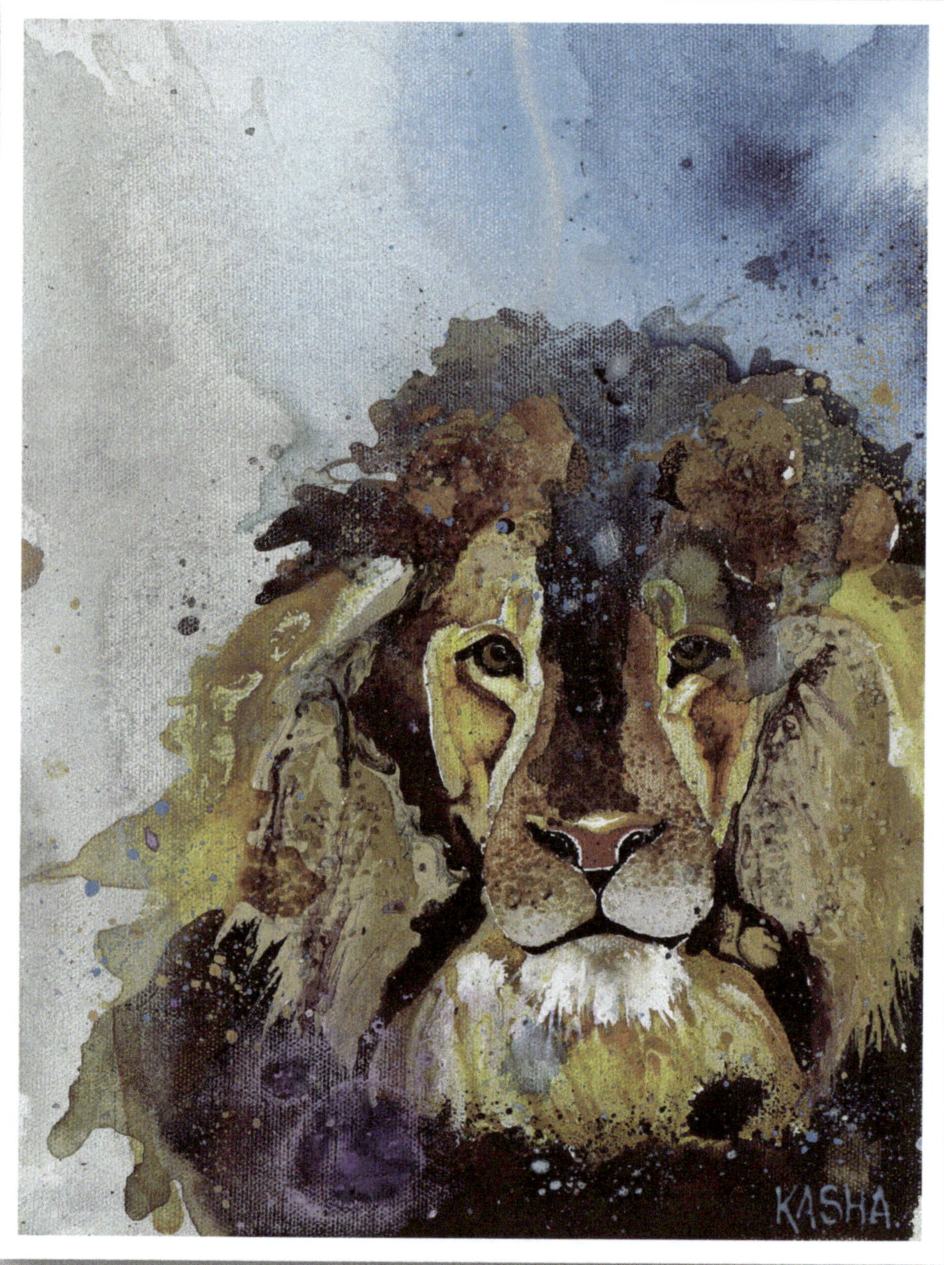

Molly-mae 12" x 9"

F·E·W
BOURBON WHISKEY
ITALIAN WINE BARRELS
46.5% ALC./VOL. 93 PROOF
KASHA

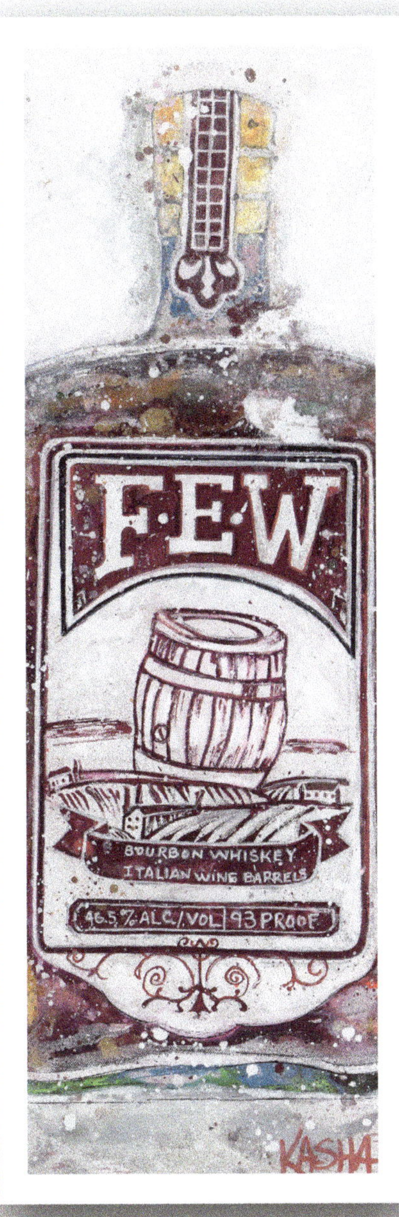

Few 30" x 12"

6

INTUITION: YOU KNOW MORE THAN ENOUGH TO START

The artwork **Few** was a piece full of information. So much going on with its label: the words, the small lines, shapes, and negative space. It was easy for me to overthink, over-draw, overdo, with my knowledge of how the label should look. How it *should* look is rooted in apparent knowledge and can feel forced. How it *does* look to me in the moment is knowing. This is a different kind of intellect but an important, innate one.

The artwork **Molly-mae** is a small piece that screams sweetness. It all works. I remember painting this and hearing myself say "Less is more, that's enough." Where I wanted to push through with more lines, I did less, and it worked. Here again is an an example of how we tune in to our intuition and work with the art to bring it to life. Intuition sometimes feels a bit easy because we were taught to try hard in order to be worthy. But the ease of intuition needs to be appreciated and allowed to work in our world.

It's as reliable as our inhale and exhale once we learn to trust it.

You need-not have deep insight to produce your art. You need knowledge of your capacity to trust your intuition. This knowing or intuition is under-appreciated and it's something we all have as a voice we hear or a gut instinct. It's being pulled in a direction. It is the core of our natural intelligence, and it is enough.

Intuition is the foundation for all other information we take in. When we start off creating art, we are convinced we need more education, instruction, and input. While some input will teach you tricks of the trade, which are incredibly helpful, too much information will overload a subtle sense of what you already know. The more you tap into your own knowing, the more you guide yourself. An overload of outside information can dilute your unique creative perspective.

This knowing will become necessary in other areas of your work: choosing tools, your approach, your system, whether you'll add or subtract something, and when you know you're finished. To be able to access this intuition, to tune into its feedback, is beneficial. As you begin to do this you may feel silly listening to something that is not in physical form. Please allow some room for possibility here because the artwork you will create is also not yet in physical form, yet you know it exists.

It's important to know that you are not your artwork. In

the end, creating your art is an experience you had, and a conversation you shared. You are still the same person of value regardless of how the work turned out. This is how you show up braver and more powerful because you are not offended by negative comments nor are you inflated by kind remarks. You hear them, but you stand apart from the words. This is vital for longevity in the field. To be able to sustain your ability to work, you must recognize you have a job to do, and while doing the work is an aspect of who you are, it's not you. This is important because one day you may choose not to be an artist. If you have built a great person along with some great artwork, then you can walk away secure in your true identity.

Simple Steps to Enable Your Intuition as You Make Your Art:

1. **Write:** Jot down what worked. When something was clear, and you acted on it, and it produced a good result, note it. This is a roadmap to where you are going, and information for your future book.
2. **Basics:** Each of us can be an artist. If we can print or write cursive, we have the ability to use lines and draw, because letters are little pieces of art. We know the foundation of color because we've all used a box of crayons. Layering colors and learning through that is building off the basics. There are eight rules of design

that we know on a subconscious level. We use them when we draw, but we probably don't know why. They are *layout, hierarchy, contrast, alignment, balance, repetition, proximity,* and *space* — and what they mean is where you put something on canvas and how big or small it is in relation to everything else. In the end, this amounts to: does it look right to you? If it looks and feels right, it is balanced and probably has these rules of design hidden in the work.

3. **Enough:** Be aware of how everything you do adds or subtracts from your work. More color on the canvas removes blank space, and too much time staring because you are afraid to do anything subtracts from your work time. Rushing a piece because you are not enjoying it can add extra work later to undo an overemphasis in one section and under-emphasis in another. Sometimes leaving it alone is the answer, and other times avoidance leaves the work wanting.
4. **Informed:** As you learn from books, videos, or even classes, consider it a suggestion. Just because another artist does their work a particular way does not mean you have to adopt that way entirely. Becoming informed is better done in small amounts, leaving plenty of room for you to incorporate your unique way of working.

Small, Useful Steps to Do Now:

1. **Speed:** Try painting faster and continuously. Have five to eight canvases lined up, ready to go. Set a timer and allow fifteen minutes per piece to finish. This will force you to use what you know and will limit your ability to stop and think. The goal is to get comfortable moving in your intuition.
2. **Photograph:** Take a picture of your painting and look at it with a fresh eye and a kind critique. This is to see it in a new way that you might not have noticed while painting. Often photographs change our perspective. See if you can add or take away anything.
3. **Boundaries**: Set guidelines as to how you make your art. This imparts the freedom to be creative without being overwhelmed with the idea that anything is possible. Limitless creativity can lead you on tangents that may feel like creativity, but when taken too far, can be avoidance. These guidelines enable deeper work because you aren't distracted, and will mirror other areas of your life. Your artwork habits and the rest of your world overlap in many ways once you start noticing them.

End of Chapter Checklist:

- ☑ **Need-not endless information** to find direction, simply settle into your knowing. We all know certain things about ourselves: I know I can focus on that, or I know I'm uninterested in that. This knowledge is what you carry with you to find rhythm in your artwork.
- ☑ **Need-not hesitate** because you don't have an answer to a creative question, simply stay in motion. Whether you draw that line to the top or center doesn't need to be overanalyzed; you can move it later or leave it as part of the work's story.
- ☑ **Need-not overemphasize** what you need to learn. This can stop you from working. You will know more as you create. Some intuition will come from books, videos, art classes, and play. Some will stem from within, and you'll be shocked because you knew it all along but were afraid to admit it. This intuition is part of your recipe for art, one that you will tweak, but will serve as your soup stock or foundation.

Love the art you saw in this chapter? Hang it up in your house and get one here:

Few: https://kasha-ritter.pixels.com/featured/few-kasha-ritter.html
Molly Mae: https://kasha-ritter.pixels.com/featured/molly-mae-kasha-ritter.html

" It's not that you absolutely positively know what to do. It's that you absolutely positively know what you can't live without."

Kasha Ritter

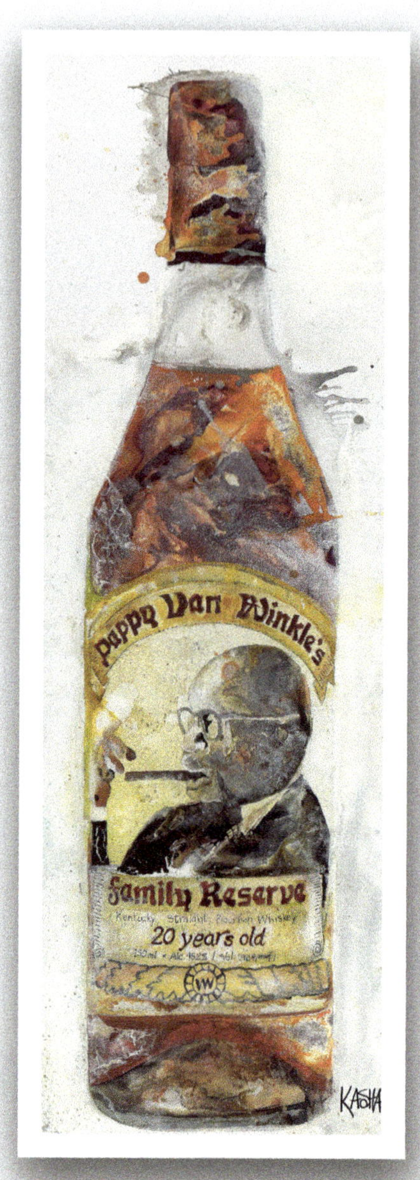

Happy Pappy 36" x 12"
© 2016 Kasha Ritter

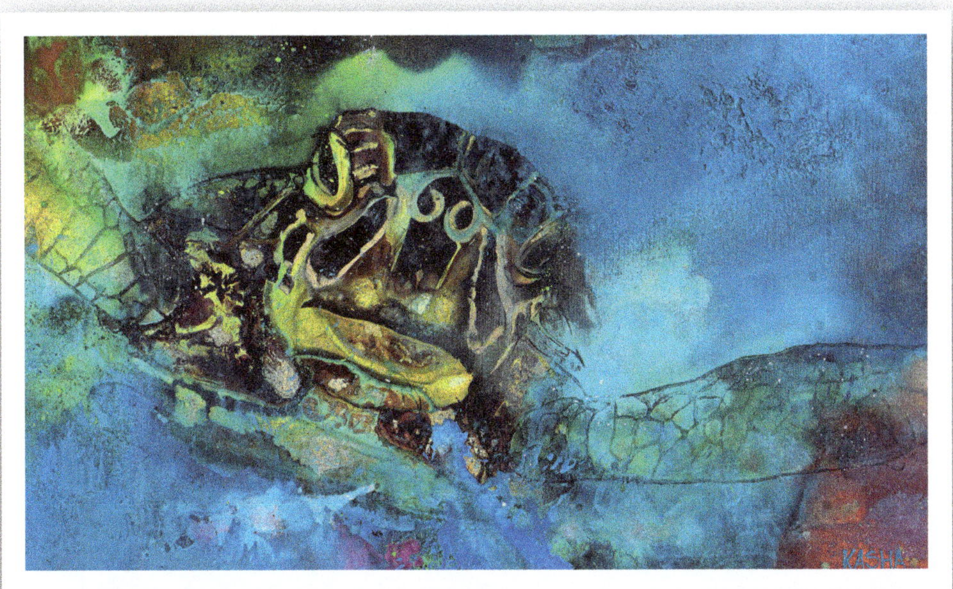

See. Turtle. 36” x 60”

7

MANAGEMENT: HOW TO CUT OUT THE MIDDLE MAN

The artwork **Happy Pappy** has paid for itself, earning money many times over. When I painted it, I paid close attention to important details but started to get hung up on his face, cigar, and hand. I wanted them to be perfect, but knew that when I overwork a piece, it blows up and the energy dissipates. I could feel this piece had a balanced energy even though it was imperfect. Here's where we side-step the ego and allow the work to flourish. This is a tremendously popular piece and prints of it sell monthly because it has good commercial value. People might not be able to buy a bottle of Pappy but they can buy a print of it, which makes it a worthwhile investment for both the artist and customer.

The artwork **See. Turtle.** a painting of a sea turtle, was a huge investment. Heavier canvas, many layers of ink and color, and so much back-and-forth playing with it. I had invested so much time, money, and thought into this piece that when it was done, I envisioned it on the cover of a magazine. I was in love! Yet this piece has not done well commercially. Emotionally it was fulfilling and work-wise it was rewarding. This is not a right or wrong situation, it's an awareness. If your goal is to have an art business, then you need to think like a businessperson and handle your work with a business mindset. Solve a problem. Meet a need.

You need-not a manager to run the business of your art, you need only to educate yourself on basic business practices. There's a sweet belief that if you focus on making art, a fairy godmother will discover you and make you a millionaire. If this has happened to you, congratulations, I look forward to reading your book. For most of us though, it's going to play out differently. We need to learn how to run a business because this is our business, and we are responsible for all aspects of it. The same attention to detail you give your paintings needs to be applied to your bookkeeping and finances. Even if you plan on creating art as a hobby, you will still have expenses and a budget and should know how much time and money your artwork costs. For example, you could spend months, layers of color, and hundreds of dollars on a painting that could have been smaller to sell for more income.

I've painted numerous equine paintings, and I do adore horses, but I painted them because I thought they would be easier to sell. We lived in Louisville, KY, where the Kentucky Derby is the event of the year, and I thought if I painted what people loved, there was a better chance to sell the art. Consider this approach and fill a need in your area. Good design solves a problem. Good art entertains, informs, or inspires. If you love to ski, paint ski-themed artwork and reach out to businesses near resorts. Love restoring old cars? Paint the cars and find your customers at car shows. Love music? Paint instruments or hands playing instruments. Love flowers? Talk to local florists about carrying your floral work in prints or greeting cards.

Once you've finished the artwork, have it professionally photographed for an online portfolio and future prints to sell. Keep these files organized and back them up on an external hard drive. Protect and preserve your work. You might feel silly at first, believing your work is too basic to have value, but that basic art is part of your story, which has tremendous value.

You can sell your art on many online platforms. I use Fine Art America. I load my art images into my account and choose the amount of profit I want to make on a print, a canvas tote, or coffee mug. I promote my website with FAA on social media and I can also send customers there if they want a print. FAA will deliver and ship. Once a month I receive a direct deposit into my business account for any sales. Selling your work will look different for everyone. Some people love to travel to art shows to build a client base. Others prefer selling through Fine Art America, Etsy, or their own website. You can sell locally at galleries or all the above.

However you sell, look for a good fit so it's sustainable.

I have a lovely, longstanding relationship with Revelry Boutique Gallery in Louisville, Kentucky. They were kind enough to give me a start more than a decade ago. What I love about them is that they give artists a chance, they offer suggestions about what might sell better, and they work with you on pricing, enabling you to make a profit. Their goal is mutual happiness and success. They care. They see I care. This is a respectful working relationship where we honor and trust each other. However you choose to sell, remember it's teamwork. You want a happy customer and store owner. They should want you to be happy working with them, too. Happy customers and store owners return to work with you when you create excellent work, are easy to deal with, and honor deadlines. Treat others how you'd like to be treated is a solid guideline. Honor your work as a professional artist and act accordingly. When you do your best work and are your best self, your customers, stores, and community will find you. What you are looking for in life is also looking for you. Align yourself to your truth.

Simple Steps to Manage Your Art Business:

1. **Finish:** Have a checklist for what you do when you finish. You have a system to start your art, and you need one to finish. Write it down. Stick with it. It might look something like this:
   - Take photos of your artwork with your phone for social media.
   - Name the art, write down its size and the year, and tape that information on the back.
   - Get it professionally photographed for your files.
   - Spray it with a protective sealer and wire it for easy hanging.
   - If you're shipping it as an order, have a system of how you wrap it. What do you include in your packaging? (a receipt, small gifts).
   - If your goal is to sell online, load it into those accounts, and then promote it on social media.
   - Don't lose steam once you finish. That's not the end game if you are in the business of art, it's the beginning of the second half.
2. **Bootstrap:** Make your money work for you. Buy art supplies you can afford. Create art. Price it for profit and put that back into your business. Build from that.
3. **Pricing:** There's a simple formula that many artists use. Take the length of the artwork and multiply it by the

width. L x W. Take that and multiply it by $1.00 - $5.00+. Start small. When you are a new artist, it's important to sell and get your work into the world but still make a profit. Using less expensive art supplies might be a way to balance this out. As you build an audience you can increase your prices. You can also make judgement calls with a sale; this is YOUR business. I remember giving an elderly woman a huge break on the cost of a painting because the artwork reminded her of her pet, but she was on a strict budget. You are building relationships, your reputation, and an income, so find a balance that brings you joy. Give of yourself when you can.

4. **Helpful:** Be of help. Don't sit back and wait for stores or customers to reach out. Touch base with the gallery owner to see if there's anything you can do to help sales. Rotate artwork? Promote them on social media? Reach out to communicate without adding anything to their to-do list. I send a brief monthly note with a sticker to people who have purchased original artwork. I do this because I LOVE stickers and they're fun, but also to let them know I'm here and painting if they might need anything. It's also a thank you to them for supporting this life I have with art.

Small Useful Steps to Do Now:

1. **SBA**: Reach out to your local Small Business Association for a support network. Meet with an advisor, take a class, explain what you need, ask for help, and get informed.
Here are some suggestions from my attorneys at Erik M. Pelton & Associates, PLLC:
2. **Company:** Name your business. Get it registered with the state as an entity (for example, a corporation or limited liability company) or as a "DBA" (doing business as) name. It's not only smart, it shows you are a professional. If you are unsure where to start, contact an attorney or your state's business website to assist you in the process. Note that protecting the use of the name for a business is different from the use of a name for a brand (even though sometimes the names match, they do not have to). If you intend to use the same name as your brand name, you will have to apply to register the mark at the USPTO separately (typically without the LLC or Inc. designation you have to include for the state filing). See below for more information about trademarks. Examples: XYZ, Inc. could be the business name, while the service offered by the business would be under the XYZ trademark. or XYZ, Inc. could offer its services under the ABC brand name.
3. **A Copyright:** is a type of intellectual property protection that covers all your original creative works. Copyright

prevents others from directly copying, distributing, displaying, or making derivatives (think printing your work on a coffee mug to sell) your work without your permission. Once created, your original work immediately qualifies for protection. However, in order to pursue legal action for infringement and receive damages (money), you will need to register your mark with the U.S. Copyright Office. There are additional concerns if you are commissioned or create the work in conjunction with another artist or company. It is always wise to put things in writing if ou are working with others or on behalf of them, and you should look at engaging an attorney to make sure ou are taking the necessary steps to protect your work. Additionally, though not legally necessary, it is best to include a proper copyright notice consisting of the copyright symbol, year of creation, and name of owner) (for example, © Kasha Ritter 2021) underneath all of your works.

4. **A Trademark:** is for your brand name, (which can be the same as your business name but does not have to be), logo, or tagline/slogan. Think of Apple® or look at your art supplies, Windsor®, or Faber-Castell®. When deciding on a trademark or a brand name, be sure to do at least a search of the internet to ensure that no one is already using that name in a related industry. Coming too close to someone else's trademark (even if not an exact copy) could be infringing on their mark,

meaning they could potentially take legal action against you. A trademark attorney can also assist you in this and can search government records to ensure there are not similar, already registered trademarks at the United States Patent and Trademark Office ("USPTO") that would provide a bar to you getting a registered trademark. Additionally, try to pick name that does not describe your products or services. Though descriptive trademarks can be sometimes be registered, they are weaker legally,and you want to pick a strong name that sets you apart from others.

Once you've decided on your trademark, it is best to engage an attorney to register the mark with the USPTO. If you receive registration, you will get nationwide protection and the ability to stop others anywhere in the United States who later start using a confusingly similar name for similar goods and services. The registration also serves as an asset that adds value to your business and demonstrates you take your venture seriously. Protecting your intellectual property protects you and your artwork and discourages others who might think of infringing on your work.

Open a business banking account for your business. Track all of your incoming and outgoing expenses. Keep business costs/spending separate from your personal spending. Get yourself an online bookkeeping service if you can afford it so you can focus on your work. Get business insurance. General Commercial Liability is a good place to start. You want business insurance to protect yourself because mishaps can happen. For example, your booth at a trade show blows over and damages another artist's work or injures a customer. Or you're delivering a large piece of art to a client and it's windy so the art flies out of your hands and cracks their car window. Things go wrong, so protect yourself. You absolutely need insurance. Budget for it.

Respect the business end of your art as much as you respect creating it. It all matters.

5. **Simple:** Build slowly. It's easy to get overwhelmed with having to design a website and build pages for multiple social media platforms. I love the rules of 3's: pick three that work for you. When you post, post in threes. And to start off, just post three times a week. Start small to avoid burning out. There is no rush. There is simple, steady building which will also be more enjoyable for you and will keep you in the game.

End of Chapter Checklist:

- ☑ **Need-not feel inadequate** about managing your business. You may not know everything, but you can learn. Get help. Get it done. It won't be as fun as creating art, but it will give you a tremendous sense of comfort and confidence. In the beginning, when I asked for help, my opening lines were "I've never done this before. This is all new to me. Can you explain to me how I…" People understand that. We have all been there. Someday you'll help someone else. Just ask.
- ☑ **Need-not neglect the business end of art.** Prioritize taking care of the books, cleaning out old emails, organizing art photos, and updating customer lists. Pick one day a week or every two weeks and devote a day to these things. While creating feels more rewarding, perfect artwork does not make a perfect art business. Producing art costs money, so you need to know where your money is going and if it's working for you if you want to continue producing art.
- ☑ **Need-not be something else.** Sometimes there's the belief that as a business owner and artist, you need to be more of a saleswoman, more charismatic, more provocative or elusive. I suggest you be honest. Be yourself. Meet people as a human being. People will sense if you are being untrue or insincere. This all comes back to who you want to be and who you want to attract.

What kind of person and business are you, and what kind of community and customers do you want to work with? Who you are, what you are, how you feel, what you have to say, how you create your art, and what you value is enough. You are enough.

Love the artwork in this chapter? Grab yours here:

Happy Pappy: https://kasha-ritter.pixels.com/featured/happy-pappy-kasha-ritter.html
See. Turtle. : https://kasha-ritter.pixels.com/featured/see-turtle-kasha-ritter.html

" You're making memories or you're making nightmares"

Kasha Ritter

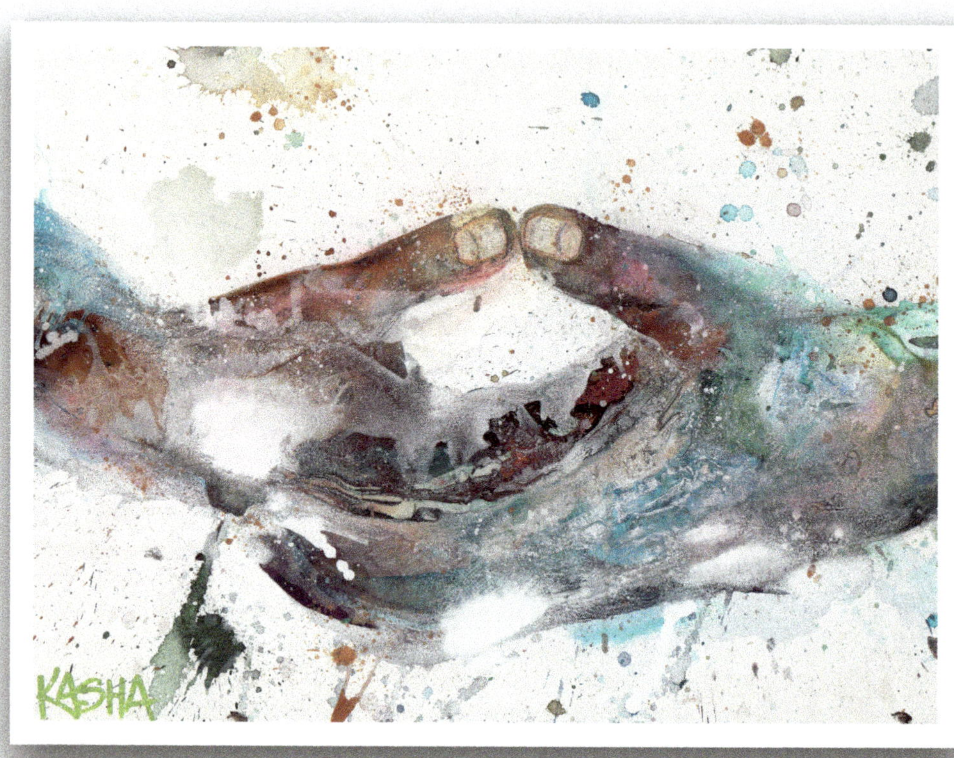

Twiddling Thumbs 18" x 24"
© 2019 Kasha Ritter

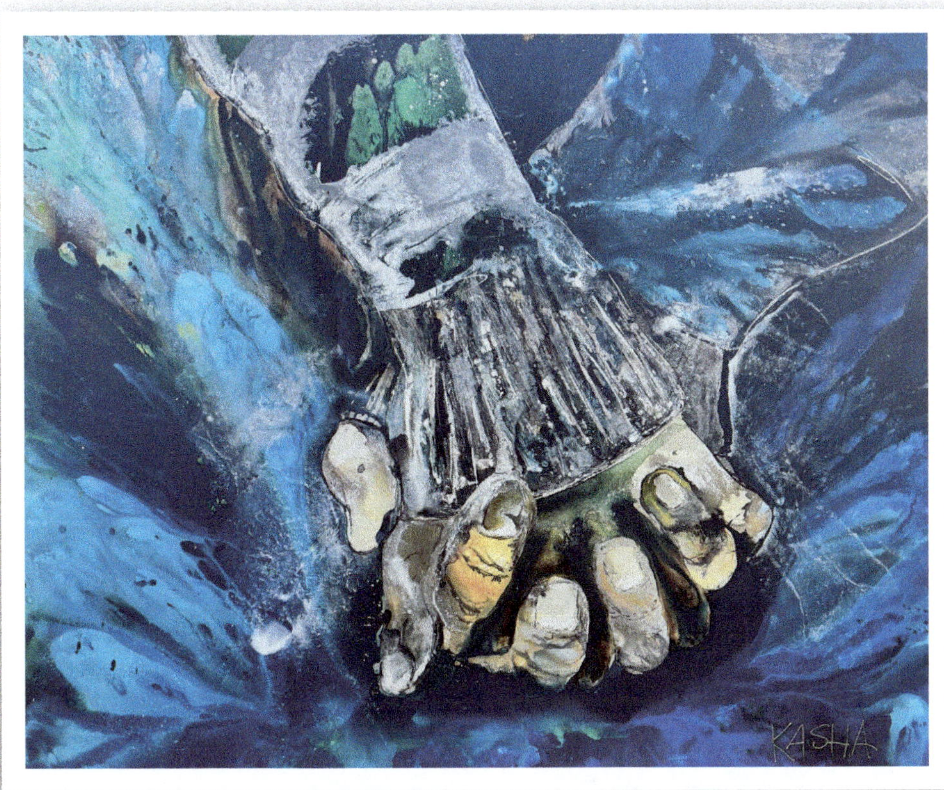

Stand by Me 48" x 60"
© 2012 Kasha Ritter

8

FAME: YOU DEFINE YOUR SUCCESS

The artwork **Stand By Me** communicates my feelings about my life with art. I have felt someone was always holding my hand. At times, my grandmother is here in spirit, and many times it is the art itself. Other times, encouraging friends, creative therapists, and body practitioners have assisted my creating through their impact on my world. Over a lifetime, my dear family as well. One definition of fame is widespread recognition. It's important to remember all the connections we created along with our recognition, especially the close ones that have steadied us through the years. Fame is an aspect of reputation and reputation is built within the safety of supportive relationships. We have received and we have given through the making of our art and the people who have stood beside us. We are better for it. The process demands it; it asks us to focus, believe, work hard, trust, and be proud of our part in the experience.

The artwork **Twiddling Thumbs** is a vision of what success feels like. Complete. Calm. Peaceful. You work but it's not forced or stressful. You have time. The art works with you, your life works with your art. This can be attained by knowing what you value and understanding the core conditions you build your work upon.

You need-not fame to consider yourself a successful artist. You need to define your interpretation of success. Fame is a label the world gives you, but success is yours to name. When we're young we think of success in diverse ways. A fireman, policewoman, doctor, teacher, movie star, investor, musician, or professional athlete are deemed successful by kids. When we are young we think freedom equals success. As an adult, life shifts for us — now we have our freedom, and now we can decide what success is for us.

Think ahead to your eulogy. Don't shy away, it's inevitable. What will they say about you, your life, and your work? What would you say? What did you do when you had the freedom to choose? Why did you paint art? What made you express with artwork? What did you hope to attain? What did you do with it? Your actions extend back to those who have come before you and reach forward to those who are watching what you do. This belief that your life sincerely matters and that what you do lives on after you are gone, brings your meaning of success into focus.

From a young age, I was very aware of the struggles the women in my life endured. My great-grandmother, Babci, arrived on a boat from Poland as a teenager for an arranged marriage. She married a difficult man, lost one child, and raised many more. My grandmother, Nanny, pointed me in the direction of art as an outlet. She never drove a car and was content to stay at home and pray. Though we never talked about it, I sensed she was anxious, doubted herself, and felt unsupported. She once told me she couldn't wait to die; she found life that tiresome. My own mom devoted her life to her children, then ended up battling debilitating illnesses later in life, which has been an incredible burden for her. I observed these women closely. I watched how they handled life, what they made with their hands, their endless dedication to their work, and their expectations of themselves and others. My respect for them is immense.

I paint for these women. I am who I am because of them. I am *of* them. I am brave, bold, and sure of myself because I saw them being these same things in different ways. They gave of themselves; they managed households and they showed love for their work and their families in their own way. They were also artists in that sense. They created their worlds.

I am continually aware of the effect my actions may have on others watching me, as an artist and business owner. As a young girl, I remember looking for female role models who resonated with me and embodied the kind of woman I wanted to become. As humans we look to others for inspiration, we watch how they do things, learning from their successes and failures. I hope to be a good role model for kids and anyone who is trying to find their own path. Many people have knowingly and unknowingly supported me along the way. I hope to give that back.

My inner circle, my husband and three children, have been integral on my path. Their unwavering support has been instrumental. My appreciation for these humans is boundless. A good family unit will support your dreams even if they don't understand them. My ability to define success on my terms stems from their ability to believe in what I do. Their presence in my life can be witnessed in my work. My relationship with them continues to fuel my expression on canvas. I'm eternally grateful.

One of the definitions of success is; "The correct or desired result of an attempt." Let's strip it down to "The desired result of an attempt." This makes it necessary to know what you desire as you start your life with art. However long or short that journey may be, remember it is your art, your work, your desires, and your definition of success. Make it authentically you and find peace and pride in it.

Simple Steps to Define Your Success:

1. **Decide:** Think about your idea of success. Not anyone else's, not what you were told from family, but your own. Post these words around your art space. Keep them in mind as you create. Instill them into your work. This is so wonderfully unique to us all, but it's also what makes you speak to the work.
2. **Respect:** We often battle our innate qualities, yet they're instilled within us for the purpose of doing good. Respect that aspect of yourself. We dole out respect to others easily yet not always to ourselves. Respect who you are, what you do, how you paint, what you create, and what makes you feel successful.
3. **Adjust:** As you grow with your artwork, you will need to adjust your definition of success. At first, it may mean finishing a piece and liking it. Or making a very small profit on a painting that you had to sell yourself. Eventually, success could be charging more for your work because you are investing in yourself. Success might look like moving away from a work situation that's no longer working. Allow yourself to adjust as you go.
4. **Free:** Free to be! And do, and to not do. Free to be confused. Freedom is something we ache for growing up. We cannot wait to stop having people telling us what to do. When we finally have that freedom, we can feel like we're treading water. We see all of the things we could

do, but we're uncertain, so we stay put. Don't lose sight of the incredible gift of being *free*. Having a multitude of choices shouldn't render you powerless. Call upon your vision, direct it, and make your dreams come true. Those same dreams you had when you dreamed of being free.

Small Useful Steps to Do Now:

1. **Remember:** Think back to when someone had a positive impact on you. A family member you clicked with who treated you like a person and not a kid. A coach in school who called out your potential when you were coasting. Women who inspired you by doing what needed to be done with grace. Pin up a photo, write their name, post it in your art space and remember them before you start working or when you get stuck. Let that remembrance carry you through to where you need to go.
2. **Honor:** Honor is personal, which is what making art and being an artist is all about. As a new artist, you might assume that what you have to say has no value, so you hesitate to bring it. What you have to say has tremendous value. Honor what it is that you are pulled to do. Respect what you need to say. Speak your mind and honor yourself.
3. **Pride:** Take pride in all the small things you will do as an artist. Sitting down to work can feel like a monumental accomplishment. Focusing during a challenging portion

of the work should be applauded. Staying positive when you might be stuck is laudable. Imbue your work with pride. Expression is a kind of courage you've cultivated, so take powerful pride in expressing what being an artist means to you.

End of Chapter Checklist:

☑ **Need-not wait for life** to label you with fame to be successful. Labels will come and go. They are only opinions. They don't know you. You know you. You nail down what your version of success looks like, however elaborate or humbly content. Your opinion of your work is what defines success.

☑ **Need-not be concerned** with how your success will come, what it will look like, or how you will incorporate it. Do your work, stay true to who you are, and success will embrace you. When you can fall into who you genuinely are, your work reflects that. We all know the inexplicable attraction of authenticity. Let that show in your work.

☑ **Need-not limit your success** out of a fear of magnificence. Creating art asks that you step into the light with dignity and step out of the way to allow the work to be seen; then to step back into the vision that created it. Remembering you are not your work, but are a *part* of the work, enables a beautiful humility. You can feel responsible for its voice. As your work speaks, those who resonate with it will find you. This is a pattern in life: things take root, they bloom, change the landscape, and beautify the surroundings. Holding yourself back benefits no one. Be brave for your work.

Did you love the artwork in this chapter? Add it to your world here:

Stand By Me: https://kasha-ritter.pixels.com/featured/stand-by-me-kasha-ritter.html
Twiddling Thumbs: https://kasha-ritter.pixels.com/featured/twiddling-thumbs-kasha-ritter.html

"The world can't tell you
who you are. It's too busy
trying to figure that out
for itself. So do it a favor
and tell it who
you absolutely
know yourself to be."

Kasha Ritter

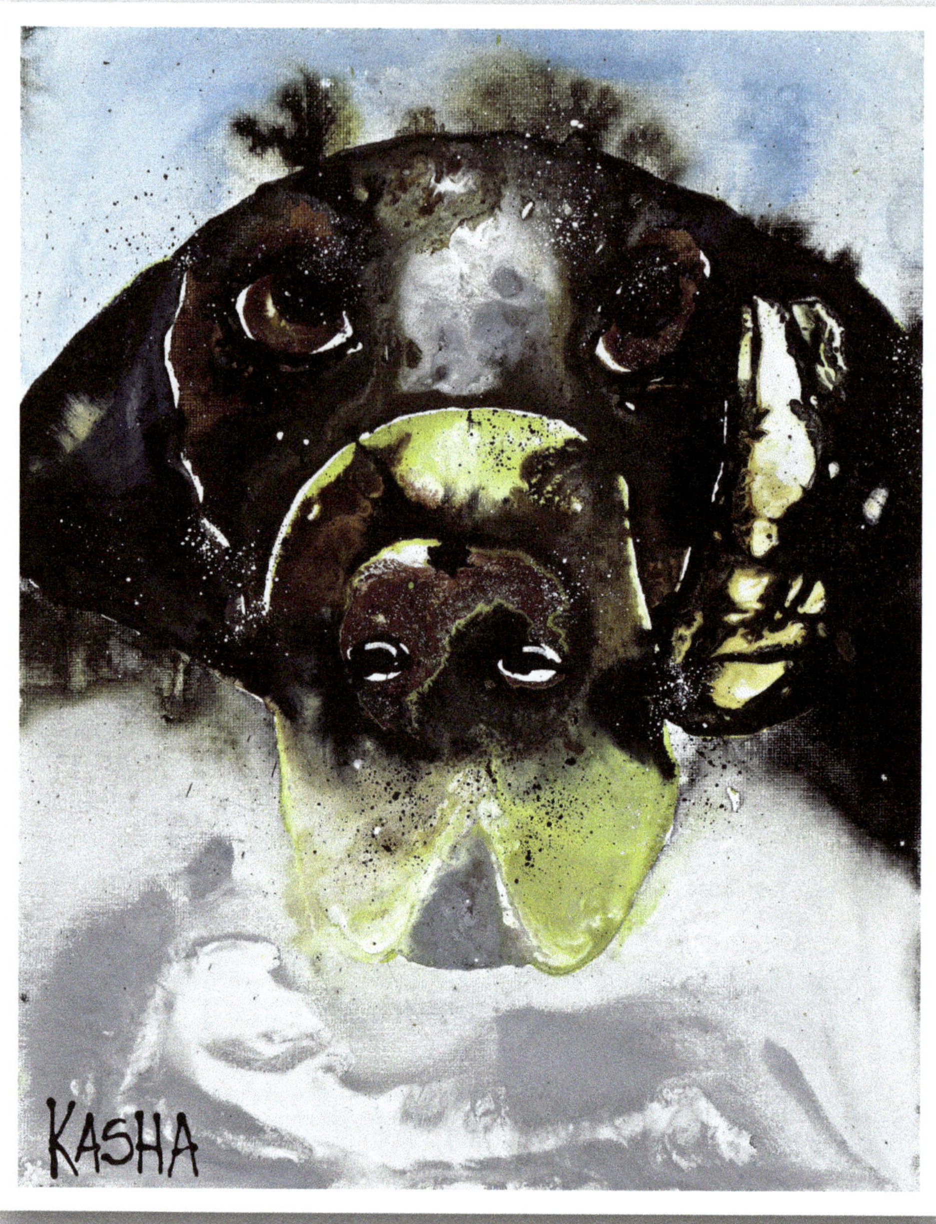

Sleep.y 12" x 9"

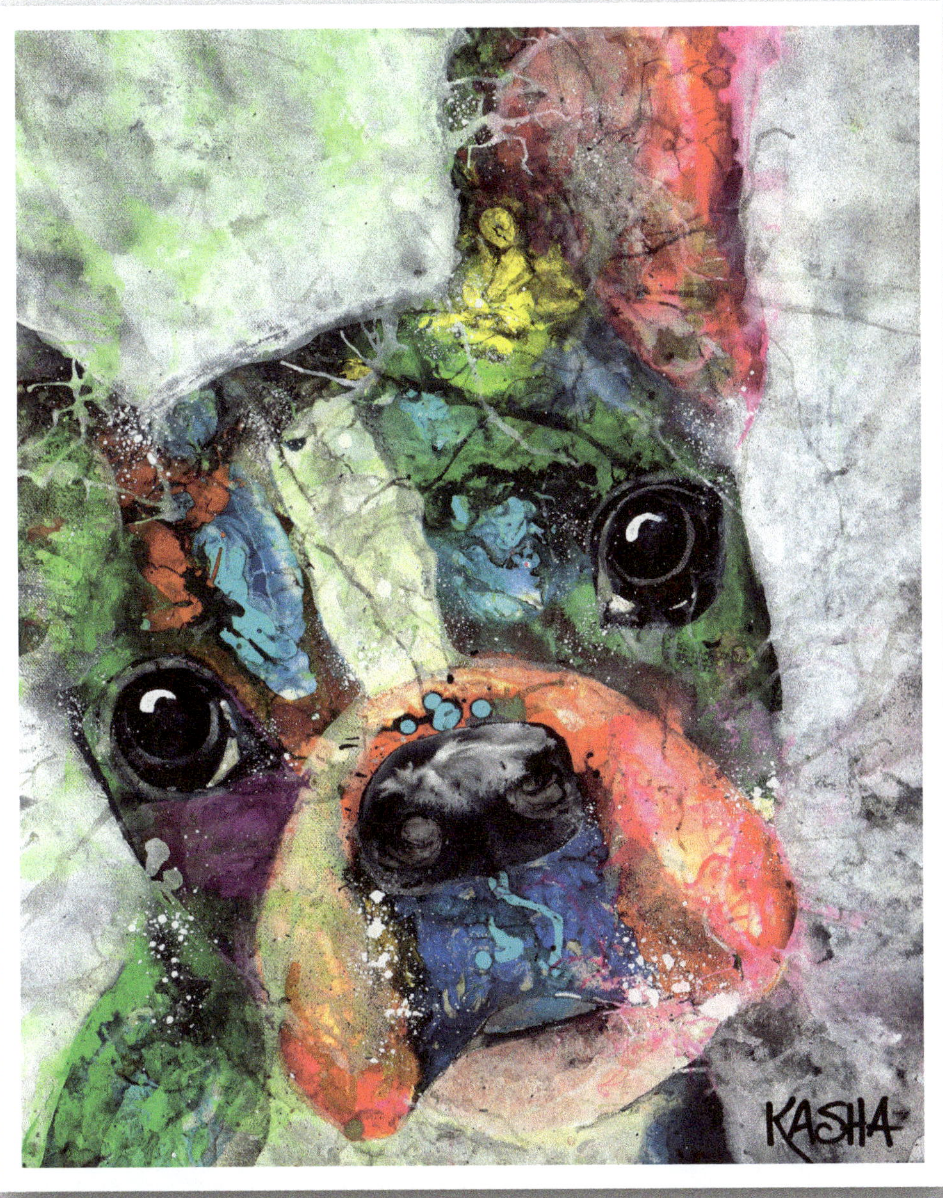

Frenchie 20” x 16”
© 2015 Kasha Ritter

9

GO FORTH AND CREATE: SHARE YOUR VISION

S**leep.y** was a struggle. I just couldn't get it going. The colors felt wrong, it refused to come together, and I wanted to be done with it. The ink blurred, the eyes weren't working, and I remember thinking, "You should have made it bluer. Why did you pick yellow? No, that's not it. What is happening here?" A steady stream of critical comments made me doubt my ability. The result? It feels uncomfortable and unsure because it was created with that mindset. I kept it and put it on my website because it's a part of my story. It taught me how to overcome those obstacles, finish, and be grateful for the experience.

Frenchie was pure joy. I hardly remember painting it. I was listening to music and would hear, "Add more pink. Now some blue. The green would look great there. Yes, that's it." I tuned into a supportive, encouraging voice that enabled me to take bolder steps with confidence. You can feel that in this painting. It feels happy! The words you speak to yourself matter. The energy you create with becomes a part of your art. Be mindful of that. Tune in to the right station.

I am quite grateful we crossed paths through this book. I hope I've provided you with some needed direction. My goal was not to solve all the problems you may encounter or to answer all the questions you may have, but to assure you that you already have what you need to start with art. Being an artist is part of who we are since we ourselves are creations. You already embody artistic creativity because you create every day. Being an artist is taking that existing creativity and applying it to paint on canvas, pencil on paper, or watercolors on a block, and is simply changing mediums. You are going from the medium of physically creating spaces in your world, to creating a picture on a flatter landscape. You know how to do this. You have been doing it your whole life.

I say to you, as Nanny said to me at the beginning of my journey, "Sit down and draw me something."

Simple steps to overcome the belief that you can't follow your dream:

1. **Be Bold:** Your art, your creativity, awaits you. It is within you, and it requires you to be bold, sure, and dependable. These qualities do not need to be extreme. Being bold may be feeling brave enough to paint something. It may be trying a new technique or experimenting with novel ways to take yourself out of your comfort zone. Stop judging and support your curiosity, much like a young child in need of a nudge.
2. **Be Sure:** Being sure might be giving yourself a deadline to finish. Honoring it may mean reaching out to prospective clients because you believe that what you do has intrinsic value. Being sure can also mean accepting rejection. No, thankful. You are sure that those people are not for your art.
3. **Be Dependable:** Being dependable can mean carving out time to create every day for fifteen minutes to establish and grow your creative muscle. It can mean having the discipline to keep at it through doubt, discouragement, or disappointment. It can mean never giving up on your desire, talents, and dream. Many paintings have left me completely frustrated by my inability to figure them out, but repeatedly coming back to them enabled me to solve the problem.

Small, Useful Steps to Do Now:

Start with three things you can do each week to support yourself on your art path. The *3, 2, 1, Go*, rule. For example, three things you will do without to make room for your art, two things you will invest in, and one project you will start. Or: three projects you want to work on, two ways you can find more time, and one thing you will not spend money on so you can move that into your art fun.

If your three things are centered on finding space and time for your art, then:

- I will set up a space for my artwork.
- I will let others know this is my space, and when I'm in it, I am not to be disturbed.
- Purchase earbuds to listen to music, a podcast, or a book for sliding into your creative zone.

Two things to invest:

- I will not buy coffee this week.
- I will skip my next hair appointment and use this money for art supplies.

One art project:

- I will paint a small canvas I can finish to feel accomplished, or I will challenge myself with a larger canvas that will take more time but I will learn more because of it.

Time Management

- I will give up 15 minutes of social media to make time for my art.
- I will give up 30 minutes of watching shows/videos.
- Pick one art project you want to tackle and can create in a week. Start small so you can start and finish to build momentum.

Reliability

- An important part of the art process is that you are reliable. Show up. Pay attention. Care enough to carry through with what you started. It matters. You are building a reputation with how you do art. This kind of consistency sets the foundation for your creative process. Respect your gift of creativity.

Creative Community

- To help you on your creative path feel free to join the **Need-Not-Artist** Facebook group here: https://www.facebook.com/groups/726298059152770

  The goal of this group is to be supportive, kind, and encouraging to all artists. You can find me on Instagram and Facebook @kasharitter. Here I'll show you the mess I make when I paint, how I paint, and how to enjoy making fun creative content. Tag me in your artwork when you post on Instagram: #kasharitter, or when you're reading this book. Definitely head over to www.

kasharitter.com and fill out the contact form. This is a great way to be included in any new happenings, and receive The Need-Not-Artist™ newsletter. It's also my way keeping in touch with you and knowing who wants to be kept in touch with.

End of Chapter Checklist:

- ☑ **Need-not permission** to step into your creativity. Please don't wait for it. There are times in our lives when we need to do what we say we are going to do. This is one of them. The permission you seek is within you. The ability to act on your conviction is also within you. This does not need to be a difficult struggle, this is a simple decision. You know you are an artist. You know you need to create. So you create. Permit yourself to act on your creativity.
- ☑ **Need-not be shy** about your art work. It does not need to be protected by you, it needs to be expressed and you are a part of that expression. Think of it as helping out the art. You are giving your work space to speak. You are assisting the work as much as you are creating the work. Sometimes when we do things for others it takes the pressure off of us and we find it easier to be fully there. Please. Fully be there for your work.
- ☑ **Need-not have an exact plan** of execution. There's a term used to describe art, known as organic. It means a kind of natural development, a way of letting things come to life, organically. When you do your work, allow room for this. Invite it to assist you. This means you may not know exactly how you will make what you want to create but, once you start the work it will develop. It will give its opinion as it comes to life, pointing

you in the right direction. The movement creates the opportunity. Allow space for this. Trust it.

Like the art above? Adopt yours here:

Sleep.y: https://kasha-ritter.pixels.com/featured/sleepy-kasha-ritter.html
Frenchie: https://kasha-ritter.pixels.com/featured/frenchie-kasha-ritter.html

"She remembered
to start the day with
"I am…."
Filling in the blanks with
what she believed herself to
be instead of listening to
people tell her
who she was."

Kasha Ritter

AUTHOR'S NOTE

As you start your relationship with art, remember that the path is not linear. This is not math or English where formulas are right or wrong. Creativity is a fluid energy. It's intuitive. You will sense something, hear a nudge, and must be brave enough to follow through. The result may not be perfect, but it will bring a new awareness. You don't have to go from point A to point B or finish one thing to begin another. It's okay to paint more than one canvas at a time. This is your art, your rules, and you are writing your book. Start where you feel you want to start. Finish where you want to finish. If you move backward, take off paint, or turn the canvas upside down to see it better, then all the better. There is not one way, there is only your way. You are finding creative solutions. Relax. Smile. Move with the art. Remember, it's okay to just try. Be kind to yourself, have fun, and let's talk soon. Here's to fearlessly creating good!

KASHA

www.ingramcontent.com/pod-product-compliance
Ingram Content Group UK Ltd.
Pitfield, Milton Keynes, MK11 3LW, UK
UKHW021836270726
14058UKWH00002B/192